The Alamo
and Other
Texas Missions
to Remember

Lone Star Books
A Division of Gulf Publishing Company
Houston, Texas

The Alamo
and Other
Texas Missions
to Remember

Nancy Haston Foster

Dedication

To my family, who've always been
there with encouragement and support.

The Alamo
and Other Texas Missions
to Remember

Library of Congress Cataloging in Publication Data
Foster, Nancy Haston.
  The Alamo and Other Texas Missions to Remember.
  Bibliography: p.
  Includes index.
  1. Spanish mission buildings—Texas—Guidebooks.
  2. Texas—Description and travel—1981- —Guidebooks. I. Title.
F387.F67 1984   917.64′0463   84–647
ISBN 0-88415-033-X

Book Design by Bernadette Payne Jeffrey
Maps by David Price

Contents

Acknowledgments

Thanks to certain individuals and staffs of these organizations for helpful information, brochures, maps, and/or photos:

Felix Almaraz, Jr., of Bexar County Historical Commission
Catholic Diocese of El Paso
Daughters of the Republic of Texas
Goliad County Chamber of Commerce
Goliad State Historical Park
Greater El Paso Tourist & Convention Bureau
Institute of Texan Cultures
C. J. Long, Alamo curator
Herbert C. Morrow of the Mission Trail Program for the County of El Paso
Bobbie G. Bego of Presidio La Bahia
Mission Tejas State Historical Park
National Park Service and staff member Santiago Escobedo
Old Spanish Missions Historical Research Library
Old Spanish Missions Information Center
Nancy Brennan of San Antonio Convention & Visitors Bureau
San Antonio Missions National Historical Park
Texas Parks & Wildlife Department and Jerry M. Sullivan
Tigua Indian Reservation
James W. Ward
Bob Washington

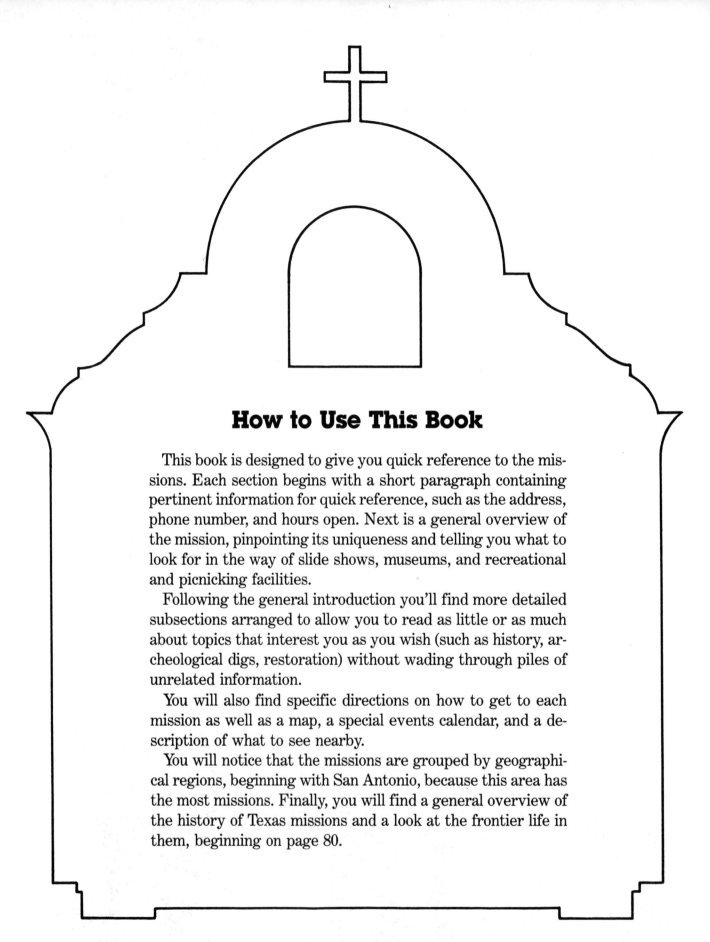

How to Use This Book

This book is designed to give you quick reference to the missions. Each section begins with a short paragraph containing pertinent information for quick reference, such as the address, phone number, and hours open. Next is a general overview of the mission, pinpointing its uniqueness and telling you what to look for in the way of slide shows, museums, and recreational and picnicking facilities.

Following the general introduction you'll find more detailed subsections arranged to allow you to read as little or as much about topics that interest you as you wish (such as history, archeological digs, restoration) without wading through piles of unrelated information.

You will also find specific directions on how to get to each mission as well as a map, a special events calendar, and a description of what to see nearby.

You will notice that the missions are grouped by geographical regions, beginning with San Antonio, because this area has the most missions. Finally, you will find a general overview of the history of Texas missions and a look at the frontier life in them, beginning on page 80.

Exploring
the Missions

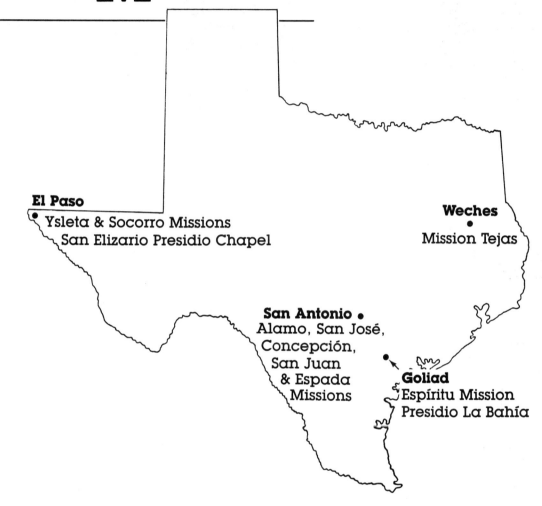

El Paso
● Ysleta & Socorro Missions
San Elizario Presidio Chapel

Weches
●
Mission Tejas

San Antonio ●
Alamo, San José,
Concepción,
San Juan
& Espada
Missions

Goliad
Espíritu Mission
Presidio La Bahía

**The Surprisingly Wild and Woolly Missions
. . . . Where the Texas Frontier Began**

Don't let the missions fool you. Rake off a layer of that pious, historic dust, and underneath lie some really tall tales not even a Texan need embellish.

Not only are the missions beautiful architectural specimens, but they harbor a lode of Texana ideal for family outings. Flamboyant combatants like Jim Bowie and Santa Anna, Indians, Spanish conquistadors and padres, Mexican and Texan revolutionaries—these heroes and anti-heroes shaped the history of the missions. What more entertaining way to get a painless dose of Texas' florid past than to learn about them?

Visit the missions and view Indian hunting tools, Spanish cannons, and ornate religious sculpture. Or camp out and take a stroll down a nature trail. These activities and more are available at some of the missions, which also double as state and national parks. This guidebook will clue you in to what you should look for and where, so that you'll get the most out of the missions and nearby sites.

This book will also provide you with some of the latest colorful revelations about elusive mission history. Archeologists and historians are constantly puttering around ruins and archives to unturn some new fact or artifact that will unravel a past mystery or debunk some myth. That's why historical markers aren't very reliable. They're written in granite.

I spent considerable time updating and ferreting out these latest theories of state and national park researchers and academics (they don't necessarily agree among themselves either!) on what *really* happened at the missions and when. It's a fascinating puzzle with new pieces falling into place continually, even as this goes to press.

For a little background, remember that these bucolic churches, these bastions of Christianity, were at times in their history hotbeds of frontier adventure, rivalry, and warring cultures. They were the sites of a veritable historical soap opera, if you will, where nations vied for empires, gold, and trade. In the seventeenth and eighteenth centuries, Spain used her missions as geographical pawns to increase her share of the New World real estate. That the tenacious Franciscan missionaries who founded them also happened to spread Christianity and civilization, well, that was just lagniappe.

The missions were again a center of action when the nineteenth century rolled around. This time it was Mexico who battled and won its independence from Spain, only to have Texas in turn fight for its freedom from Mexico's tyrannical rule. The Republic of Texas used the missions, already built like forts, as strongholds in the struggle to free itself from Mexico, which considered Texas a substate, just as the Spanish had.

The Alamo, or Mission San Antonio de Valero, is the most well-known example of a church-turned-fort and the site of the bloody conflict whose outcome engendered a battle cry known the nation over—"Remember the Alamo!"

But there was another, lesser-known yell that resulted from a battle in the vicinity of another Texas mission and La Bahia presidio near Goliad. There, the Texan forces under Col. James Fannin lost again and ended up imprisoned in La Bahia presidio, with about 352 of them being massacred. Thus the cry "Remember Goliad!" arose to inspire the Texans also.

So you can see, the erratic history of Texas' early frontier days and subsequent civilization can be traced by simply visiting and studying the missions.

To portray the missions in their heyday as always bustling with activity would be grossly inaccurate, for at times, they were dull, tranquil, and lonely outposts. Still, once the first missions were founded in Texas in the 1680s, they became the centers of colonization and thus the center of the action. For missions *were* the frontier, and their inhabitants suffered all the inherent problems of living on the frontier—starvation, drought, floods, plagues, and Indian attacks.

Missions were Spain's means of colonizing the land it had explored in the New World. Presidios, or forts, were usually built nearby to protect them, and this system had already worked in Peru and Mexico.

Since the Catholic church and royal government were intertwined, the missions were subsidized. Being beneficial to both the church and state, they served as a way of subduing the native culture, while utilizing free labor. Thus, the missions were religious and trade schools all rolled into one, used for teaching the Indians how to farm, ranch, weave, and build, while providing them with food and shelter.

While some Indians welcomed these advantages, others resented this cultural intrusion and were less than eager converts. There were frequent Indian attacks, and the missionaries were constantly having to retrieve recalcitrant runaways. But to Spain's credit, its colonization system at least provided for the original Americans. Other systems weren't so hospitable.

From the 1500s when Spaniards Cabeza de Vaca, Coronado, Moscoso, and Oñate set foot in Texas, Spain began extending its territory of New Spain northward beyond Mexico to surpass the other European powers, England and

France, which were already entrenched in eastern North America.

Spain resented France in particular, which had become interested in the Mississippi River area and landed in Texas by mistake in 1685 (La Salle). Thereafter, Spain settled and built missions near Indian villages and rivers to protect her territorial claims. From these settlements grew familiar Texas towns such as San Antonio, El Paso, Goliad, and Nacogdoches, and the rugged highways that connected them, known as El Camino Real (The King's Highway), provided a system of routes that is still used today.

Thus Spain left a large, undeniable footprint on the Texas landscape. Those dedicated Franciscan missionaries, along with the military and

This weather-beaten, sculptured stone entrance is the doorway to Texas' most historic lodestone, the Alamo.

civilian settlers, brought with them ranching and irrigation systems, a legal system, and a colorful language, all of which still exert a profound influence on the Texas culture.

Another legacy left us by the Spanish missionaries is the endearing mission architecture itself. These fine old Spanish colonial churches (most still Catholic parish churches today) give a comfortable, patined texture of antiquity to the state. When viewing the missions, remember those old walls reverberated with not only ecclesiastical chants, but Indian yells and war whoops. Not only used for holy rituals, these missions have also been cattle pens, army headquarters, private residences, and mercantile stores. A lot of humanity has trundled through them over their centuries-old existence, and it's this motley cast of characters and their arresting tales that make the missions unfailingly intriguing.

San Antonio Missions

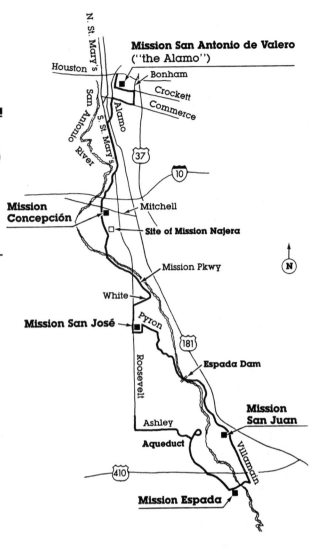

San Antonio is akin to an old, tattered history book, and there is probably no better place in Texas to experience Texan and Spanish antiquity. The city and its surroundings "runneth over" with old Spanish missions. In fact the city is the only one in the nation with five missions in its limits, four of which compose the San Antonio Missions National Historical Park.

After all, since Spanish padres and officials first happened upon the local river and named it San Antonio de Padua (after St. Anthony) in 1691, the area has been an arena for power struggles, battles, and political peccadillos. San Antonio itself was founded only a little while af-

ter New Orleans in 1718 and has a lively historical pedigree to match that of the Louisiana city.

The most well-known mission, the Alamo, anchors downtown San Antonio. Indeed, in the beginning it *was* San Antonio. It and the other missions sprang up, along with the presidio (fort), as a convenient way station to the older missions in East Texas, where Spain was attempting to protect its real estate from France. In time, the San Antonio missions would eclipse the ones in East Texas and become more successful, probably because they simply were closer to the headquarters of New Spain (in what is now Mexico) and because the Coahuiltecan Indians were more amenable to being "civilized." In fact, three East Texas missions had to be abandoned and relocated here (as Missions Concepcion, San Juan, and Espada) because of bad relations with the Indians and the French.

The other mission here, San Jose, grew to become one of the flagships of the Spanish mission chain and is often touted as the "queen of the missions." Its architectural beauty and its large restored compound make it one of the best examples of a frontier Texas mission. After the Alamo, at least take in San Jose if you don't have the time to see the rest.

But of course, before seeing any other Texas mission, you must see the Alamo. It is a whole story by itself. Though that saga is often embellished by tale-spinning Texans and free-wheeling novelists, it is enough to say that in 1836 a small, courageous band of men fought a bloody battle here and bought precious time for the fledgling Texas republic to later win its independence from Mexico.

The Alamo is conveniently located in central downtown San Antonio. From there, get a mission tour brochure and map from the Visitor Information Center across the street and make the tour of the other four missions by car. They are all located in south San Antonio, and blue and white Mission Trail signs point the way. The whole tour will take roughly a morning or an afternoon, but you might want to opt for a picnic lunch outside the missions grounds or at nearby parks. To follow the Mission Trail signs, go south on Bonham (the street on the back or east side of the Alamo) a couple of blocks, then turn right on Commerce. Get in the far left lane so you can turn left at the next street, South Alamo. Continue on South Alamo, and you will

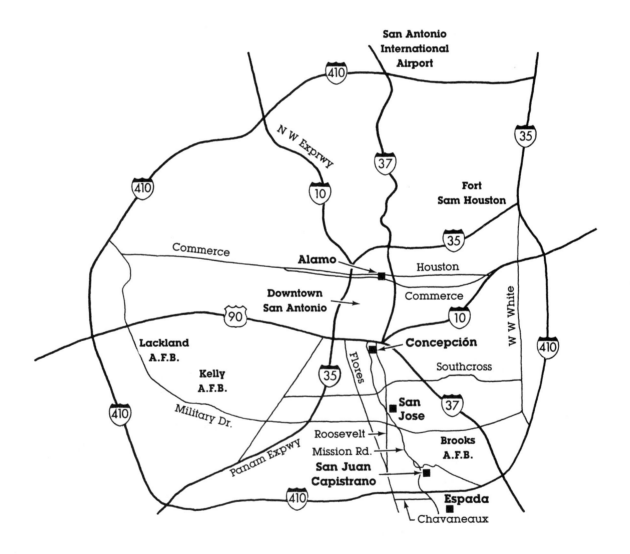

begin to notice the Mission Trail signs that will lead you to the rest of the missions.

These four missions are run by the National Park Service and are officially called the San Antonio Missions National Historical Park. (There are no camping facilities here.) The Alamo is operated separately by the Daughters of the Republic of Texas. All are admission free and open daily.

There are other options for touring the missions. Several commercial bus tours leave from in front of the Alamo daily. See your hotel or the Visitor Information Center for details on cost and tour companies.

One of the most interesting times to visit the San Antonio missions is during La Semana de las Misiones (around August 6), a whole week of festivities held annually at the various missions. The celebration includes festivals, music, food booths, speeches, seminars, and religious services.

Don't forget the other sightseeing treats in San Antonio. This is tourist mecca, with both historical and recreational sites. See "What to See Nearby" in the section on the Alamo.

Visitor Information Center
    300 block of Alamo Plaza (across from the Alamo)
    San Antonio, Texas 78205 (512) 299-8155

San Antonio Convention & Visitors Bureau
    P.O. Box 2277
    San Antonio, Texas 78298 (512) 299-8123

San Antonio Missions National Historical Park
    Office
    727 E. Durango
    San Antonio, Texas 78206 (512) 229-6000

VIA Gray Line Sightseeing Tours
    P.O. Box 12489
    San Antonio, Texas 78212 (512) 227-5251

The Alamo

Mission San Antonio de Valero

At Alamo Street and Houston, on Alamo Plaza, San Antonio/Museum and Souvenir Shop/Open 9 a.m.–5:30 p.m. Monday–Saturday; 10 a.m.–5:30 p.m. Sunday/Free/(512) 225-1391

The Alamo has had more tales spun about it than has Brer Rabbit. And the battle there has been so popularized by historians and Hollywood that the legends and myths tend to obscure the fact that it started out as a peaceful mission.

Yet this old war-horse of Texas Independence wears well with time. That battle where a band of 187 men died fighting off a Mexican army of thousands *is* the stuff that legends and heroes are made of. Even today, in the midst of downtown San Antonio, surrounded by retail stores and bustling shoppers, the Alamo still stirs the heart of many a Texan seeing it and that bright red, white, and blue Texas flag flying proudly over it. In fact this is one of the most popular historic landmarks in the nation, attracting some 2 to 2½ million visitors annually.

Passion, violence, and courage were found here in the men fighting for what they believed in, against hopeless odds. The Alamo saga *is* the narrative of rough-hewn men like Jim Bowie, Davy Crockett, and William Travis, who thought "Victory or Death" preferable to a Mexican dictatorship. Of course, the Mexican government held quite a different viewpoint; they took umbrage at upstart colonists wanting their country's land.

But this battle (actually it was a siege that lasted thirteen days; the battle itself lasted only about three hours) played an important role in history. It bought time for Sam Houston to gather a make-shift army to defeat Santa Anna, the president-dictator who led the Mexican Army at the Alamo and later at the Battle of San Jacinto. That decisive victory brought Texas independence from Mexico in 1836.

Did you know that old Sam actually ordered the Texans to blow up the Alamo before they abandoned San Antonio, because he didn't think the mission could be defended? Fortunately, or unfortunately for the Texas defenders, they didn't pay any attention to him.

Once Texas got its freedom from Mexico, it was annexed by the United States in 1845. An ensuing border dispute resulted in the Mexican War (1846–1848), which gave America title to lands that eventually became Arizona, California, Colorado, Nevada, New Mexico, and Utah.

The Battle of the Alamo

What led to the battle of the Alamo? Well, basically it's the familiar story of people revolting against a tyrannical government.

Prior to 1836, Texas was an administrative substate of Mexico, and many Texas inhabitants were colonists from the United States accustomed to more democratic rule. These Texans did not care for Santa Anna's dictatorship; they wanted to rule themselves.

The Mexican government felt otherwise and thought that the colonists should abide by the rules of the country whose land they inhabited. Since many adventurers and free spirits mi-

This familiar postcard look of the Alamo is the view you see from the gates of the convento patio.

grated to Texas, the stage was set for revolution.

A small clash at Gonzales, southeast of San Antonio, started things off in October 1835. About this time, Santa Anna sent his brother-in-law, General Martin Perfecto de Cos, to take command at San Antonio. Cos was soundly defeated by some Texan volunteers led by Ben Milam (hence the slogan "Who will go into San Antonio with old Ben Milam?") and sent packing back to Mexico.

This act infuriated Santa Anna, and he vowed to return to San Antonio to avenge the humiliating defeat. A most uneven grudge match was about to begin.

Why was it so uneven? Many of the Texans who had captured San Antonio went home because they thought the fighting was over once Cos had surrendered and pledged never to fight against Texas again. Only about 104 volunteers remained at the Alamo.

The revolution was not an organized effort at this point, and only now was Sam Houston trying to muster an army of volunteers. Hearing that Santa Anna was amassing thousands of troops, Houston sent orders by his friend Jim Bowie that the Alamo's guns be taken and the walls blown up. Houston felt the Alamo could not be defended by so few men.

But Bowie didn't agree with Houston, and somehow the Alamo never got blown up. Shortly thereafter, William B. Travis, sent by Texas' provisional governor, Henry Smith, arrived on the scene, and there was a power struggle over command. But Bowie was sick with typhoid-pneumonia, and Travis ended up with the unenviable job of commanding an untenable defense.

Santa Anna's siege of the Alamo began February 23, 1836, when his demand that the Texans surrender was answered with a cannon shot. (An eighteen-pounder capable of firing such a shot is still on the Alamo grounds.) For twelve days the battle was mainly an artillery duel, because the Texans not only had more cannons than the Mexicans, but they also had sharpshooters with better guns.

During the siege, Travis penned a famous letter carried out by courier Albert Martin to the town of Gonzales (Travis' letter became renowned later as its stirring contents were published in U.S. newspapers and the Texans' cause told):

At the arched walkway on the Alamo grounds is a cannon that was presented by Mrs. Albert Maverick.

Commandancy of the Alamo
Bexar, Feby 24th 1836

To the People of Texas and all Americans in the world—Fellow citizens and compatriots—I am besieged, by a thousand or more of the Mexicans under Santa Anna—I have sustained a continual Bombardment & cannonade for 24 hours & have not lost a man—The enemy has demanded a surrender at discretion, otherwise, the garrison are to be put to the sword, if the fort is taken—I have answered the demand with a cannon shot, & our flag still waves proudly from the walls—*I shall never surrender or retreat. Then,* I call on you in the name of Liberty, of patriotism & everything dear to the American character, to come to our aid, with all dispatch—The enemy is receiving reinforcements daily & will no doubt increase to three or four thousand in four or five days. If this call is neglected, I am determined to sustain myself as long as possible & die like a soldier who never forgets what is due to his own honor & that of his country—

Victory or Death

William Barret Travis
Lt. Col. Comdt.

Travis had already requested help from Colonel Fannin and his Texan troops at the Goliad

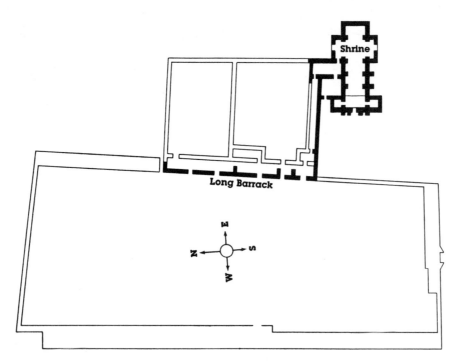

Probable layout of the Alamo at the time of the 1836 battle. Note that the square was in front of the church (shrine) or to the west on into what is now Alamo Plaza. (Courtesy of C. J. Long.)

garrison, but to no avail. Desperate, he sent another courier. Again Fannin failed him, having started out with several hundred men but turning back. Only the town of Gonzales answered the call, sending 32 men and boys, who slipped in between enemy lines.

On March 5, the Mexican cannon bombardments became so threatening that Travis called together his men and gave them the choice of fighting or trying to escape. Legend has it that he drew a line on the ground with his sword and asked all who would stay at the Alamo to cross it. Only one man, Louis Rose (nicknamed "Moses") bucked peer pressure and chose to escape. Though scorned later by historians, he had had a good deal of military experience, having fought with Napoleon, and he realized the futility of the project. He also lived to tell of it.

The next day on March 6, the assault came around dawn. With bugles sounding the dramatic "Deguello" (no quarter to the defenders), the Mexicans attacked on several fronts. But it wasn't till they regrouped and hit the north wall that they succeeded in penetrating the Alamo's defenses.

After only about three hours, the battle was over, for how long could 188 hold out against an estimated 1,500 to 2,500 troops? The number of troops for both sides is still debatable, but the best current guess for the Texans is 188 (one man is thought to have escaped). It has been estimated the Mexicans had up to 5,000 men, though their reports show a much smaller number actually participated in the attack.

Travis fell across his cannon with a shot through his forehead. Bowie died on his cot, with pistols spent and knife bloodied. Only about sixteen noncombatants on the Texas side survived, mainly women and children. Historians dispute the number of Santa Anna's losses. Estimates range from 300 to 1,500 men, depending upon which side's reports you read. The General sent one of the Texan survivors, Susanna Dickinson, wife of Captain Almeron Dickinson, to spread the word of the Alamo's demise to the Texans.

Mrs. Dickinson was in a room in the church when the Mexicans came in during the fighting. She related that they killed two little boys and " . . . I saw four Mexicans shoot (a man named) Walker and stick their bayonets into his body and raise him up like a farmer does a bundle of fodder with a pitchfork when he loads it onto a wagon."

Santa Anna had the Texans' bodies piled high and burned in a pyre.

The Alamo's Other Lives

Although most famous as a battlefield, the Alamo has led nine lives, spanning several centuries. It's been everything from a fort and hospital to an Army depot and mercantile store selling groceries and booze. But it began as a peaceful mission in 1718, a date the city of San Antonio calls its founding date.

Mission San Antonio de Valero, as it was originally called, was founded more or less as a halfway station for the Spanish on their way to missions in East Texas from Mexico. The route these missionaries took was the beginning of El Camino Real (The King's Highway), later called the Old San Antonio Road to East Texas.

A Spanish expedition of officials, soldiers, and friars first stumbled on the area in 1691. They named it and the local river San Antonio de Padua, because they made their discovery on that saint's day.

Later a Franciscan missionary, Fr. Antonio de San Buenaventura y Olivares, requested and received permission to establish a mission in the newly discovered San Antonio area. Told to relocate the failing San Francisco Solano mission, which was near what is now Eagle Pass, to this new area, Fr. Olivares did so and renamed it San Antonio de Valero. (The Valero part shrewdly honored the Viceroy of New Spain, the Marquis de Valero.)

Fr. Olivares first set the mission up on the west bank of the San Antonio River near San Pedro Creek, a little northwest of the mission's present location. It was moved in 1719 to the east bank of the river and then again in the 1720s to its present location, upstream. It served as a mission to the Indians until 1793 when it became the first Texas mission to be secularized. Most of the state's missions had begun to fail, and the Catholic Church began to close them down. Therefore San Antonio de Valero's lands and tools were parceled out to the Indian inhabitants.

At its peak period as a mission, in the 1740s and 1750s, the Alamo had about 328 Indian inhabitants; a farm and an acequia to irrigate the fields; a ranch with cattle to the northeast; textile, carpenter, and blacksmith shops; a granary; a friary; and a chapel. The church part that we recognize today was begun in 1744, though it was never fully completed, and the upper part later collapsed.

After the Catholics closed down the mission, a Spanish cavalry unit from the Mexican town of Alamo de Parras occupied the abandoned compound in the early 1800s, and people started calling the place El Alamo. (Alamo means cottonwood tree.) About this time the old friary at the Alamo was also used as San Antonio's first hospital, treating both soldiers and civilians. Later came the Mexican troops who used the place as a fort, and in 1835–36 the Texas revolutionists made their heroic stand there.

After the famous Battle of the Alamo, the place lay vacant a few years, until the Republic of Texas deeded it back to the Catholic Church. But again it reverted to military use when the Church leased it to the Army in 1845 as a quartermaster depot. The Confederates took it over during the Civil War, and then it was occupied by the U.S. Army until 1876 when the Army moved to the new Fort Sam Houston.

About this time, a merchant by the name of Honore Grenet bought the property with the friary (or long barrack) on it and added a frame second story. In this august historic site, he sold groceries, dry goods, boots, whiskey, tobacco, and produce. He also leased the old Alamo church from the Catholic Church to use as a warehouse!

Following Grenet's death, a notice about his estate offered the store property for sale, together with its lease of the Alamo, by proclaiming:

> The location on Alamo Plaza ... with the street cars passing it every few minutes during the day and until late at night makes this one of the most eligible business sites in San Antonio. This property will prove to be a Genuine Bonanza to its purchaser or lessee.

Well, the Hugo and Schmeltzer Company couldn't pass up this bonanza, and they turned the barrack into a department store. Fortunately, the State of Texas finally stopped some of this nonsense and bought the church part from the Catholic Church in 1883. However the enterprising businessmen hadn't given up on the commercial value of the property with the long barrack. In 1903, they tried to turn it into a hotel site. Clara Driscoll helped the Daughters of the Republic of Texas forestall this event by buying the property herself and letting the state repay her later. The state then gave custody of the whole property to the DRT to be maintained by them at no charge to the state—which they have done ever since. Thanks to them and Clara, we don't have an Alamo Hotel overshadowing the historic church.

Architecture and Restoration

In its heyday as a mission, the Alamo was situated much differently than it is today. It had a walled square typical of Spanish missions, but it wasn't the one you see around the church today. Instead of enclosing the church, the walls were built in front of it to the west. The church was just an adjunct to the *convento patio* and *convento* (now the long barrack), which faced on the square.

The missions, as mentioned earlier, were used by Spain to colonize the area, giving the Indians both religious instruction and skill training. Each had to be a self-supporting unit, and the Mission San Antonio de Valero was no exception. The compound included the aforementioned carpenter, blacksmith, and textile shops.

(The Indian women wove their own fabrics and clothes.) And there were rooms built into the walls of the square for the Indians to live in.

The earliest structures were simply huts of adobe and straw. Later on more permanent structures of native stone were added, though many buildings of adobe were still used. All of these disappeared through deterioration, battles and time. The only original structures left are the church and part of the walls of the convento, and even these have undergone changes.

The present church structure was begun in 1744 (the keystone is dated 1758). Even the top of this one, however, was blown away during a storm in 1762. It was never repaired or finished before the mission was shut down in 1793. The Spanish cavalry unit that was later stationed in the abandoned mission in the early 1800s (and gave the mission its current name) put a roof on the church. But this was removed by General Cos in 1835 when he was fortifying the Alamo. He piled the debris from the roof against the back wall and used it as a dirt ramp to roll cannons up on.

The big battle of 1836 didn't help the Alamo's architecture any either. It was left to the new lessee, the U.S. Army, in 1849 to restore the convento and rebuild and reroof the church. The credit for the distinctive curvilinear gable top of the front facade goes to Major E. B. Bab-

The Long Barrack Museum houses archeological artifacts and Spanish and Texas Republic era items.

These outer walls of the Alamo compound encompass the Long Barrack, which earlier served as the convento where the friars stayed.

bitt, who was in charge of the restoration. The Army also added the two upper windows.

It wasn't until the 1930s under the aegis of the DRT that the church's vaulted ceiling and roof were installed. The DRT also acquired more of the property around the Alamo, and through the WPA the area was cleared, a wall surrounding the block added, and a museum built.

Now, for a little more detail on the Alamo's architecture. The church is cruciform in shape, with the two arms of the cross originally planned for side altars. The ceiling is vaulted, and there are side rooms for the sacristy, confessional, and baptistry. The floor is flagstone and the walls are of irregular stones (mainly native limestone). In short, the building is of simple design, with only the front facade having a decorative character. The front is called a retable facade, which like the altar of a church, has niches to display statues and religious objects. It is in an early Baroque style, with floral designs and scalloped shell patterns surrounding the huge wooden doors.

While the Alamo may have the similar stone construction and the general Spanish colonial aesthetics of other missions, it really is atypical in that it has no bell tower. This can probably be accounted for by the top collapsing back in 1762 and altering its appearance; it is thought that it had twin bell towers and a dome back then.

What to Do and See

Cenotaph

A gleaming white marble monument, dedicated to the Alamo heroes by the State of Texas in 1936, fronts the Alamo at the corner of Houston and Alamo Streets. This cenotaph was done by the sculptor Coppini.

The Alamo Grounds

The Alamo today is a walled-in compound, taking up an irregular block in downtown San Antonio. After all, the mission was the original settlement, and the town grew up around it.

On the grassy, treed grounds are several buildings, the most obvious one being the church with the familiar postcard facade associated with the Alamo. Along with the Long Barrack Museum walls, the church is the only original part of the Alamo left standing, and much of it had to be restored. The other buildings, the Museum/Souvenir Shop, the Daughters of the Republic of Texas Library, and the meeting hall have been added in more modern times. They are constructed, however, to blend in with the aged look of the original Alamo structures.

The Daughters of the Republic of Texas are the patron angels of the Alamo. They've been

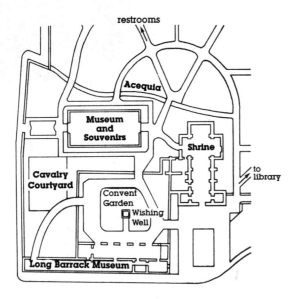

Present layout of the Alamo grounds.

taking care of it for the State of Texas, at no cost to taxpayers, since 1905. And they don't charge visitors either; admission is free. One way they support their effort is through selling giftshop/tourist items.

The DRT keeps the place spick and span, and colorful flowers and plants bloom year round. These landscaped grounds are a pretty place to stroll downtown even if you aren't interested in history—particularly on a sunny day. There is usually a breeze, and there are several cannons throughout the grounds for the kids to climb on. (And the new, clean restrooms are located on the northeast wall.)

Museum, Exhibits, and Slide Shows

All three public buildings on the Alamo property have exhibits. The church itself has a few tastefully scattered about, but it still retains its somewhat hallowed atmosphere.

After taking an obligatory picture of the front of the Alamo (the trick is not to include ten strangers walking by), enter the church, or the "Shrine" as the DRT likes to call it.

It's not quite as quiet as a library, but things are more subdued in here. After all it was a church. (No photos are permitted inside.) Inquire at the information desk about the free guided tours that last about 30 minutes. If you want to tour it on your own, ask for a guide sheet and mosey around the exhibits—they are pretty self-explanatory.

The small room to the right as you come in the front entrance is the baptistry; the one to the left is the confessional. The larger rooms to the left were probably the sacristy. Now they are called flag rooms because they contain flag exhibits.

Around the church walls are display cases with interesting little items like Crockett's beaded buckskin vest and his rifle "Betsy," a Bowie family knife, and Travis' estate records. There is also a long rifle (called the Dickert rifle after its maker) actually used in the defense of the Alamo, as well as a model of the Alamo as it appeared in 1836. Paintings of Davy Crockett, William Travis, James Bowie, and James Bonham hang on the walls.

After viewing the exhibits in the church, go out the back door, take a left, and walk past the big tree and well in the courtyard. In the corridor in front of the Long Barrack Museum (this is not the same as the Museum/Souvenir Shop you saw as you came out of the chapel) you can see a ten-minute color movie about the Alamo battle. The screen is awfully small, but the movie isn't bad.

Also in this same corridor you should look for the display on Clara Driscoll, who helped save the Alamo property, and a model indicating where archeological excavations have been dug at the Alamo. Inside the Long Barrack Museum some artifacts from these digs are displayed—pot sherds, musket balls, coins, and gun flints.

Also inside the museum are two self-operated (just punch the button) slide shows that last only a few minutes. One is on the Alamo's history; the other is on the battle. Other exhibits include such things as flintlock rifles, Republic of Texas currency, early Texas tools and pewter, a Spanish conquistador helmet, arrowheads, and my whimsical favorite, a replica of Davy Crockett's coonskin cap, worn by John Wayne in the movie *The Alamo*. (Apparently, the cap utilized all of the raccoon—eyes, head, and tail.) Next, visit the Museum/Souvenir Shop, where the kids can purchase coonskin caps and replica Bowie knives or Remember-the-Alamo belt buckles and dominoes with armadillos on them.

This is more gift shop than museum, but there are display exhibits in the middle of the large one-room area. One is full of early guns such as derringers and Colt pistols; the others contain barbed wire, tools, and Sam Houston memorabilia.

Texas History Research Library of the DRT

This pleasant library of the Daughters of the Republic of Texas is open to researchers, not the browsing public. Located in the southwest corner of the Alamo complex, it has books, maps, documents, manuscripts, periodicals, clippings, and photographs pertaining to Texas history, in particular the era of the Texas Republic. Photographic reproduction and duplication services are available.

Archeological Digs and Finds

The Alamo has long fascinated archeologists, and in recent years they have uncovered a skull thought to be from one of the battle participants. It isn't known if it is a Texan or Mexican skull, only that it appeared to be that of a twenty-year-old male.

Over the years, the Alamo has been the site of many excavations, beginning with the one dug by the WPA in the 1930s in the area east of the church and the Long Barrack where there were commercial buildings. No records of their dig have been found.

Since 1966, all archeological digs have been documented and the artifacts collected. Some of these (pot sherds, musket and cannon balls, Spanish coins) are displayed in the Long Barrack Museum. A model exhibit outside the museum indicates the locations of these Alamo digs.

Here's a brief list of the excavations:

1966 The Witte Museum did excavations on the north side of the Alamo church in the convento patio areas. They uncovered the remains of perhaps the original north wall of the second patio or some other remnant of a structure in the North Court. Also in the Well Court, they found the remains of what appeared to be a room. The wall base was made of large adobe bricks.

1970 The Texas Archeological Survey excavated north of the DRT Library and uncovered nineteenth-century structural footings and part of the mission acequia.

1973 More excavations in the North Court were done by the Witte Museum. They uncovered the remains of what is believed to be the original walls of the convento patio and also of what appeared to be wall footings of four rooms.

1973 This dig by Thomas Hester of the University of Texas at San Antonio (UTSA) was east of the Museum/Souvenir Building and verified the location of the old acequia ditch.

1975 The Center for Archaeological Research of UTSA excavated in the small park in Alamo Plaza, trying to locate the mission quadrangle south wall. The damaged remains of the wall footings were found.

1977 When the City repaved Alamo Plaza, its backhoe trenching just outside the front wall of the Long Barrack (convento) was monitored. It was determined that the present restored wall does indeed sit upon the original convento wall.

1977 Excavations were again carried out by the UTSA Center for Archaeological Research when the City replaced the flagstone paving in front of the church. Datable cultural items retrieved from the stratified soil levels and the church's foundation were studied. Also a palisade ditch dug as a defense during the Battle was discovered along with many battle artifacts.

1979–80 Probably the most intriguing item that has turned up is the skull found by the UTSA Center for Archaeological Research team while digging near the wall in the North Courtyard. Tests indicate it is apparently the skull of a 1836 battle casualty. Found near musket balls and a gun lock, it belonged to a male of about 20, who probably died by the sword or a similar weapon.

Excavations done on the west side of Alamo Plaza during River Walk linkage construction uncovered remnants of the old mission quadrangle west wall and rooms.

For archeology devotees, more detailed information can be found in reports published by the UTSA Center for Archaeological Research on some of the more recent digs. The Museum/Souvenir Shop sells them.

Refreshment Break

No food and drink are allowed in the buildings, and none are for sale there. But you can go out to Alamo Plaza in front of the Alamo and buy an ice cream bar or raspa (snow cone). Unfortunately, lately there have been too many entrepreneurs hawking their goods to tourists and cluttering up pretty Alamo Plaza. You can eat in one of the several lunch counters and hamburger joints across the street, or for a more pleasant meal, take your taco or sandwich in the fresh air of Alamo Plaza with its old-fashioned gazebo, park benches, and shade trees. You will find yourself sitting in the lap of history, for even the merchant and hotel buildings around the Plaza are old. (The venerable Menger Hotel dates from 1859.) There are, of course, many restaurants in the area within a block or two.

Timing Your Visit

If possible, avoid seeing the Alamo when everyone else does, on weekends and holidays. It's a pleasant place for an outing anytime, but more so when the tourists aren't swarming.

The Alamo's landscaped grounds make for a pleasant downtown stroll. The Museum/Souvenir Shop is in the background.

How much time should you allow? You can easily go through the whole thing in an hour, but you should leave some time for sauntering around the landscaped grounds. This is the essence of San Antonio, being able to stroll in a green, tree-shaded area, listening to the birds sing, while surrounded by a teeming city.

Where do you go from here? You need only look out the front door of the Alamo. Tour buses and horse and carriages jostle for tourist business. Take one of the buses for a tour of the other four Spanish missions in the city, or drive your own car on the Mission Trail mentioned in the San Antonio introduction.

Directions to the Alamo

The Alamo is conveniently located in the middle of downtown San Antonio. Most of the freeways take you downtown, but the closest one to approach the Alamo from is on the east side of the central business district, and at this point is called both IH 35 and IH 37.

Get off on the Commerce Street exit and go west for four blocks until you reach Alamo Street, Take a right on it, go north two blocks, and you're at the Alamo and Alamo Plaza. There is no special parking area—you'll just have to scramble for a meter or a commercial parking lot. The Alamo occupies an entire block at Alamo and Houston Streets. Officially it seems to have no address, but it is in the 300 block of Alamo Plaza.

Tours

Free guided tours of the Alamo are given to the public daily, usually on the hour at 10, 11, 2, 3, and 4. They last about 30 minutes. Ask at the information desk in the church when the next one is scheduled.

Annual Events

Since the Alamo practically has to beat off visitors with a stick, there are no festivals held here. And too, because the DRT doesn't like to overcommercialize the historic site, most of the events that take place at the Alamo are serious, patriotic ceremonies. But now and again, a bit of frivolity slips in, such as at Fiesta time, when the city has a ten-day celebration around April 21 (San Jacinto Day, when Texas won its independence from Mexico in 1836).

Here are some annual ceremonies:

February 22

Order of Purple Heart ceremony—It is supposed to be held on George Washington's birthday, but it may be on the alternate observed day.

March 2

Texas Independence Day ceremony—This commemorates the day Texas declared its independence from Mexico.

March 6

Heroes Day—This is the solemn observance in the church of the day the Alamo fell to Santa Anna's troops in 1836, with the DRT honoring the heroes who died with a roll call of the defenders' names.

March 17

St. Patrick's Day—Harp & Shamrock Society of Texas has a wreath-laying observance with accompanying music and celebration.

Week of April 21

Fiesta—This ten-day celebration includes many activities but those involving the Alamo are:

The Coronation of King Antonio, which takes place in front of the Alamo at night, with a lot of pomp and frivolity as the King of Fiesta is crowned midst torchlight.

The Pilgrimage to the Alamo, which is an afternoon processional parade that ends up at the Alamo to present floral offerings in honor of Texas heroes.

Week of August 6

Semana de las Misiones—During Missions Week, the opening program is presented at Alamo Plaza. This will fall somewhere around August 6, El Dia de las Misiones.

Other Sights to See Nearby

Downtown San Antonio is brimming with historic sites and entertainment areas. The River Walk, just a couple of blocks to the west, is a must-see. Shops, sidewalk cafes, and art galleries line the bustling San Antonio River as it winds its way through town. You can take a barge ride down its one-and-a-half miles of landscaped parkland.

Quaint La Villita (village), HemisFair Plaza, the Institute of Texan Cultures, San Fernando Cathedral, the Spanish Governor's Palace, and Market Square, are all within walking distance or a ride on the motorized VIA city streetcar.

For information on these sights, simply cross the street to the Visitor Information Center in the 300 block of Alamo Plaza. Also across the street on Alamo Plaza is the Heart of Texas Show, a 45-minute movie/slide show providing information about Texas—its land, people, festivities, and idiosyncrasies—right down to indigenous rattlesnake sounds. Non-Texans find it informative about the natives.

City Tours

Various commercial conveyances with guides eager to show you the rest of the city are easily found on the Alamo's doorstep. Several bus lines offer long-range city and mission tours, and a vintage streetcar along with horse and carriages will take you for a spin in the downtown area. All depart daily, some every hour on the hour, during the day.

Mission San Jose

Mission San Jose y San Miguel de Aguayo

At 3200 block of Roosevelt Avenue and Mission Road, San Antonio/Large grounds with exhibits and picnic facilities nearby/Open daily 9 a.m. to 6 p.m./Free/(512) 922-2731

Mission San Jose is the classic archetype of a Texas mission with its graceful, patined Spanish Colonial architecture. See it, if none else, to get a feel for the rugged, frontier days of the 1700s and how the resolute Franciscans built primitive oasis cities in the wilderness.

Life was severe then. If backbreaking hours of hard labor didn't shorten your life, marauding Indians or epidemics would. And this large, restored mission compound in south San Antonio is one of the few left to reflect the fort-city nature of these outposts.

"A veritable fortress" is what one friar called San Jose in 1749. "Although greatly exposed because of its location to attack by the Apaches, who have become so daring that they threaten the Presidio of San Antonio even in the daytime, they have never bothered the mission." The whole square of walls has been restored, with the church ensconsed in the middle, and there is even a mill nearby.

The chapel's beauty and ornate craftsmanship stand out incongruously in what must have been a harsh, sparse environment when the mission was founded in 1720 shortly after the Alamo. Although the phrase "Queen of the Missions" has been effusively overused, San Jose is indeed the foremost Texas mission and one of the most magnificent in the country. As such, it's the cornerstone of the San Antonio Missions National Historical Park and one of the most photographed missions.

The classic lines of the church's bell tower combined with the ornate exterior stone sculpture hark back to an era when artisans had the time to hone their craft. On a sunny day, there is nothing more inspiring than the sight of this aged Spanish colonial church, with its off-whites highlighted by the sun, contrasting with the bright blue Texas sky.

Absorb a bit of the peaceful serenity of long ago while standing on the square's flat prairie ground. Never mind the occasional traffic or jet overhead, the mission complex is still far enough away from urban hustle to give you an ideal of what secluded, pioneer life was like then.

San Jose can be seen easily in an hour, but why pass up a chance to luxuriate in this ready-made serenity? Spend half a day, and take a lunch (or buy one at the various fast food restaurants across the street) and picnic on the grounds. There's a special area with picnic tables north of the mill. An indoor refreshment room with vended snacks and cold drinks is also on the north square wall.

As of this date, limited staff precludes any guided tours for individuals. But pick up the brochure map at the mission complex entrance and follow the square clockwise to the Indian quarters, granary, official residences, mill, church, sacristy, Rosa's window, and courtyard convento, and then go back by way of the corner bastion, to see the unique way residents had of defending the walls. You'll see how the Indians lived in their apartment-like quarters, with their crude tools and utensils. Typical of most missions, there were carpenter, blacksmith, tailor, and textile shops, as well as nearby farm lands and a ranch, called El Atascoso, some 25 miles away to the southwest near the present-day towns of Poteet and Pleasanton. Have your walking shoes on—the square is almost two football fields long. There are a few exhibits along the way, and there is a large model of the mission (circa 1770s) in the granary with an explanatory narration.

San Jose is still a parish church, and if you have a chance, take in the colorful mariachi noon Mass on Sundays. The mission is also the site of colorful special events during the year, all open to the public. For instance, there are the July 4th parish festival, the Semana de las Misiones around August 6, and the presentation of the Christmas pageant, Los Pastores, in the Christmas season.

Life in a Frontier Mission

What was it like to live in the missions on the cutting edge of the frontier? How was a mission set up, and how did it work? One way to visualize San Jose then is through the eyes of a visiting church fireman, Fr. Juan Agustin Morfi, who made a report on Spain's frontier missions and toured San Jose in 1777.

It "is in truth, the first mission in America, not in point of time, but in point of beauty, plan, and strength, so that there is not a presidio along the entire frontier line that can compare with it," he writes. (Thus San Jose's "Queen of the Missions" claim.)

". . . no one could have imagined that there were such good artists in so desolate a place." Everything ". . . is in such good order and so well planned, that even if the enemy would be able to lay siege to the mission, the besieged,

This classic chapel is at San Jose, Texas' largest restored mission.

Some of the delicate stonework at the church entrance that led to San Jose being dubbed the "queen of the missions" is pictured here.

having their granary well filled with food and plenty of good water in their wells, could afford to laugh at their opponents."

San Jose in that era appeared much as we see the restored compound today. Along the square walls were the Indian "apartments" that consisted of one room and a kitchen with a fireplace. These had crude cots covered with buffalo hides and blankets woven by the Indians. As Morfi described the place further:

"There is also a loom in which rich blankets, cotton, cloth, sackcloth . . . are woven. There is a carpenter shop, a blacksmith shop, a tailor shop, and everything needed in a well-regulated community." The granary was on one side wall, with the church and convent inside the square.

An acequia or irrigation ditch flowed through the square. Outside the walls was the mission farm. It "occupies an area about a league square and is all fenced . . . For its benefit water is taken from the San Antonio River and distributed by means of a beautiful irrigation ditch to all parts of the field, where corn, beans, lentils, cotton, sugar cane, watermelons, melons and sweet potatoes are raised . . . and there are some fruit trees. . . ." continues Fr. Morfi.

And even farther away, perhaps 25 miles to the southwest, (near present day Poteet and Pleasanton) was the mission ranch, El Atascoso. All the San Antonio missions had ranches of their own, and this was probably the largest. At least it seemed to have the highest count of livestock—1,500 head of cattle and 5,000 sheep one year.

San Jose did not have the turbulent history of, say, the East Texas missions, which Spain had to abandon because of border hostilities

The original San Jose church dome collapsed due to deterioration and had to be reconstructed in the 1930s.

with the French. In contrast, San Jose has led a rather sedate life, allowing, however, for routine pestilence and Indian raids. No major battles were fought in its confines, though U.S. troops barracked there in the mid-1800s did use the lovely church facade for target practice!

San Jose was founded in 1720 at the behest of Franciscan Friar Antonio Margil de Jesus. The friar was an astute fellow who asked the governor of Coahuila-Texas, Marques de Aguayo, for permission to establish the mission and named it after him. Margil, in charge of several East Texas missions, had to abandon his missions there and flee to Mission San Antonio de Valero (the Alamo) as a temporary refugee. While in San Antonio, he decided that Spain could use another mission in the area to act as a way station to the East Texas missions when they were reestablished.

San Jose's first camp was on the San Antonio River bank south of the Alamo, somewhere near where Mission Concepcion is today. Temporary huts and adobe structures acted as its "buildings." It wasn't till a move to the present site on the west bank that permanent structures arose. There is a report that by 1749 the stone granary was finished. It still stands today and is thought to be the oldest remaining stone building in all of Texas. It even predates the Concepcion church and the Spanish Governor's Palace. Construction on the present church (an earlier stone chapel predated it) didn't begin until 1768 and wasn't completed until 1782.

The mission, which at one time had a peak Indian population of 350, was partially secularized in 1792, and part of its property was distributed to the Indian residents. By 1824 it was completely closed down as a mission, though it continued to be used for church services.

It was downhill for the mission after this. Texan and U.S. troops occasionally quartered here at various times in the 1840s–1850s, and a monastery used the place for about eight years in the 1860s. But slowly the mission compound fell into ruin. The Indian quarters and walls disappeared. Parts of the church walls collapsed, and eventually so did the dome.

It would take until the 1930s for San Jose to be restored. In 1941 it became a State Historic Site and then in 1983 part of the National Historical Park.

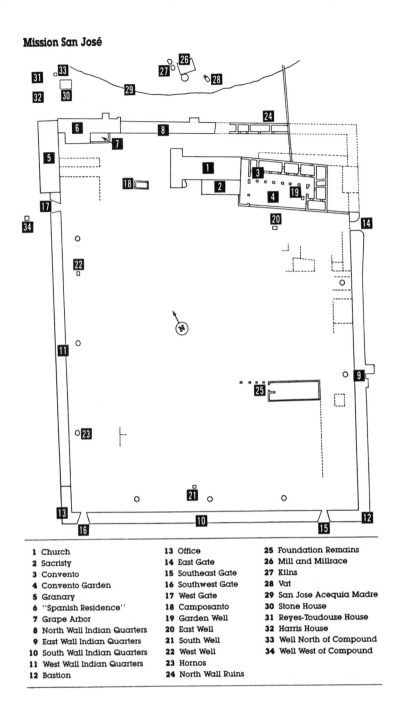

1 Church	**13** Office	**25** Foundation Remains
2 Sacristy	**14** East Gate	**26** Mill and Millrace
3 Convento	**15** Southeast Gate	**27** Kilns
4 Convento Garden	**16** Southwest Gate	**28** Vat
5 Granary	**17** West Gate	**29** San Jose Acequia Madre
6 "Spanish Residence"	**18** Camposanto	**30** Stone House
7 Grape Arbor	**19** Garden Well	**31** Reyes-Toudouze House
8 North Wall Indian Quarters	**20** East Well	**32** Harris House
9 East Wall Indian Quarters	**21** South Well	**33** Well North of Compound
10 South Wall Indian Quarters	**22** West Well	**34** Well West of Compound
11 West Wall Indian Quarters	**23** Hornos	
12 Bastion	**24** North Wall Ruins	

Self-Guided Tour Checklist and Exhibits

The park entrance is in the southwest corner of the mission. Get a free brochure map, and from there prepare for a lot of walking. The self-guided tour directs you clockwise around the square, with a detour on the north side to the mill outside the walls. There are explanatory plaques at each point. Look for these items generally indicated in this order on the map:

- Indian quarters—These consisted of two rooms, with a fireplace in one corner. Rawhide cot, pottery, and crude cooking utensils are displayed.
- Outdoor oven
- Water well—Original wells were hand dug.
- Art and industries exhibit—This includes Spanish colonial artifacts uncovered at San Jose during reconstruction, such as a hand-carved wooden cross, iron prod ranching tool,

ceramic chocolate cups, plow, yoke, spurs, and a chair back.

- Granary—At the northwest corner of compound, it could store 5,000 bushels of corn and other produce. The granary predates the church and contains a large scale model of the mission complex in the 1700s, with a narration about mission life.
- Spanish residence—Tradition has these rooms in the north wall housing Spanish soldiers early on and the alcalde later, though this may not have been the case. The alcalde's office is furnished as it might have been, complete with feather pen and ink and a huge foot-long key. Wonder what padlock this went to? The gates?
- Acequia (irrigation ditch)—This was the Acequia Madre or primary irrigation ditch of San Jose. The water was tapped at a dam on the San Antonio River and channeled to the two and one-half square miles of mission fields nearby.
- Mill—The upper mill works include the hopper, grinding stone, and controls, with the turbine below. Water powering the mill was brought by the acequia, then channeled to the crop fields. The plaque says "oldest mill in Texas," but remember that only the lower part is original; the upper is reconstructed.
- Kilns—Conical pits at the mill's side are believed to have been pottery kilns.
- Processing pit—There has been supposition that this was a sugar processing pit, but no one knows for sure.
- Church and sacristy—See "Architecture" section. The sacristy, used to store vestments and religious service items, is the only part of the compound that never fell into partial ruins.

This view of the San Jose church is from within the huge pastoral walled-in compound.

The granary at San Jose (circa 1749) was one of the few original structures of the mission to survive time's erosion.

- Rosa's Window and restored frescoes—These are on the south side of the church. See "Architecture."
- Convento and courtyard—The convento served as living quarters and offices for the Franciscan missionaries. All that remains are these roman and gothic arches and walls.
- Indian soldiers' quarters—Indians trained in defense lived near the corner bastions. They had to keep watch for Apache Indian attacks.
- Corner bastion—Defenders could survey the two exterior walls from here and fire on any attackers.
- Fortified gate—Platforms above the gates were used for defense, and the loopholes in rooms on each side enabled viewing and firing on unfriendlies.
- Decline and restoration exhibit—As of this writing, photos and text about San Jose's decline and ultimate restoration are exhibited in this area near the park entrance.

Architecture and Restoration

Don't be misled by the mission compound as you view it today. Only a small portion of all these old-looking structures is actually *original*. Much of the compound is just good reproduction work. But such a good cosmetic job was done that all the reproduction work blends in well, appearing to be weathered and several centuries old. By the 1930s when most of the restoration was done, only the church itself (its dome, roof, and some walls had collapsed), some of the convento arched walls, the granary, and the lower part of the mill were left standing.

Thanks to the tenacious San Antonio Conservation Society, which spearheaded the mission's revival by buying the old granary property in 1930, the community got behind the restoration project and utilized county, church, and private monies to fund it. WPA labor was used.

The church's dome and roof, as well as the square walls around the compound, which had completely disappeared, had to be reconstructed. The church doors had been stolen, and tourists could even buy chunks of the crumbling structures as souvenirs!

Many people, not just the friars who had a vested interest, have acclaimed the San Jose chapel as a prime example of Spanish colonial style. It has a square bell tower on the right of the ornate stone sculptured entrance, a cupola roof, and other clean, classic lines. Depending upon how much sun is out, the church may appear different colors. Made of limestone from a quarry near Mission Concepcion, San Jose appears to be greyish-white when there is little sun. With more, it becomes cream-colored.

The baroque entrance has lavish sculptured stonework—including cherubs and scrolls topped by a window balcony and cross. Naturally, San Jose (St. Joseph), the patron saint of the mission, has a prominent place in it. All this elaborate stonework frames the large carved wooden doors. The church exterior is thought to have originally been colorfully frescoed with geometric designs of bright yellows, reds, and blues. Some restored samples of these frescoes are on the south side of the church.

The graceful Rosa's Window, also on the south side of the church at the sacristy, has been the subject of much conjecture and many local tales. The window has grillwork in the middle surrounded by ornate stone-carved scrolls and foliage and for years was referred to as the "Rose Window." But architects insisted that it did not have the rose pattern of a true rose window, so someone conjured up a tale about a surveyor named Pedro Huizar sculpting this while pining away for this lost love Rosa—thus the revised name. However, recent researchers believe Huizar didn't move to the area until after the window was finished, and so he is no longer credited with sculpting it. Some now feel that

Rosa's Window, with its ornate stonework, is one of the mission's landmarks and is located on the south side of the church at the sacristy. Tales about the window abound.

the window was associated with a feast day ceremony connected to St. Rose and, thus, the name link.

Contrasting with the ornate entrance, but continuing with the overall simple design of the church, the inside worship area has off-white walls with brightly colored trim and a lack of busy ornamentation. There are wooden pews, rock floors, and candle-shaped wall light fixtures. The high, vaulted ceiling is taller than the chapel is wide. And the church doesn't follow the traditional cruciform shape either. The sacristy is on the south side and opens back to the remaining arched walls of the convento and the cloister garden.

Behind the church and north wall is an old mill built sometime between 1789 and 1794 by a Father Pedrajo. The lower level was uncovered in 1933, and the top restored by Ernst Schuchard. It was a gristmill, of the Norse type, with the turbine wheel in the chamber below.

Be sure to note the corner bastion at the southeast corner of the square walls. The bastion was built in a bulbous shape so that defenders could survey the two exterior walls and fire on attackers through wall holes. This was a standard feature on Spanish defensive structures. No wonder the Apaches gave up trying to storm the mission compound itself and resorted to attacking stragglers outside.

Directions to San Jose

Mission San Jose is in south San Antonio. If you are only going to visit it and not take the Mission Trail from downtown to all four of the missions, get on IH 37 going south and exit west on Southcross Blvd. (This intersection is a bit confusing if you are coming from downtown San Antonio. You actually exit onto New Braunfels, then take a right on Southcross.) Continue westward on Southcross until you reach Roosevelt. Take a left and go south on Roosevelt until you reach the 3200 block, where it intersects Mission Road. Turn left on Mission Road, and the park parking lot is on the left corner.

If you wish to take the Mission Trail route, see the map and instructions at beginning of the San Antonio section.

Tours

Take your own self-guided tour here, following the park's free map and informational plaques along the way. There are no staff tours for individuals as yet, but arrangements can be made for special groups.

Several commercial sightseeing buses also tour San Jose. Check in front of the Alamo, where they leave daily.

Annual Events

Every Sunday at noon
Mass—A colorful mariachi Mass is held at the church.

Late December or early January
Los Pastores—This Christmas pageant is traditionally held on one weekend shortly after Christmas. But the dates may vary.

This is the fortified southeast gate in the walls, which were built in a square shape to enclose the mission compound.

Shadows play on the remaining arched walls of the old convento.

The celebration begins with Mass at the church, followed by the centuries-old Spanish Christmas play. Local parishioners perform outdoors in brightly colored costumes and masks, with the church as a setting. Los Pastores means "the shepherds," and was used by Franciscans to teach the Indians about the Christmas story, while throwing in a good/evil plot to boot. Sponsored by the San Antonio Conservation Society (224-6163), it's performed on Saturday and Sunday evenings. There is also music, plus food booths with traditional Mexican goodies such as bunuelos (delightful crispy sugared pastry in the shape of a tortilla) and tamales. The play is performed in Spanish with an English narration. Dress warmly, it's usually cold this time of the year. Free.

July 4

July 4th Festival—This is an all-day parish festival open to the public, with mariachi entertainment, food, and game booths. There is no admission charge.

August 6

El Dia de las Misiones—Held at San Jose, this celebration honors the mission's founder, Father Margil. It usually includes a mass and activities emphasizing the religious aspects of the missions. El Dia de las Misiones (which means the day of the missions) is part of the week-long Semana de las Misiones held at all of the missions. There is no admission charge.

Mission Concepcion

Mission Nuestra Senora de la Purisima Concepcion de Acuna

807 Mission Road at Felisa, San Antonio/ Open 9 a.m. to 6 p.m. daily/Free/(512) 532-3158.

Mission Concepcion lays claim to being America's oldest unrestored stone church. Unlike most missions whose walls and innards have crumbled over the years, Concepcion was made so well it's still basically the same church it was when built in 1755. And like other Texas missions, this one also played a minor part in the Texas Revolution. A skirmish between the Texans and Mexicans, dubbed the Battle of Concepcion, took place nearby.

You'll find Concepcion first on the Mission Trail if you're touring the four missions in south San Antonio after seeing the Alamo first, and it is the closest to downtown. From here follow the Mission Trail signs south to the other three missions, all of which embody the San Antonio Missions National Historical Park.

After seeing the bustling Alamo, Concepcion (short for Mission Nuestra Senora de la Purisima Concepcion or Mission of Our Lady of the Immaculate Conception) will seem sedate. Much less commercialized, it's on a small plot, crowded and surrounded by an older section of town. But don't let that put you off. Its rough-hewn cedar post fence (the original square walls are gone) encloses a pleasant architectural refuge, providing good photo subjects in the church and convento.

Also be on the lookout for the few remnants of original frescoes painted on Concepcion's walls. These faded designs can no longer be seen in other missions. One of them, called the "Eye of God," eyes you from the ceiling! The stone church is typical of mission design, with twin towers and a cupola. Symmetrical and chaste, it has a dash of embellished sculptured stone around the large wooden doors of the front entrance.

There are no guided tours as there are at the Alamo, but get a brochure at the office entrance by the small parking lot, and take the self tour.

The original square, including the wall and Indian quarters, is long gone, as is the granary. But the convento, the living quarters of the missionaries, is still there, as are some old textile rooms.

The self-guided tour leads you through the textile workshop, where Indians wove their own material for clothes and blankets, to the patio area. In it is an old well that has never gone dry. From this point walk along the sidewalk to the church. Inside is a real delight for people who like unadulterated design. Plain, white walls are slightly accented by bright colors of ochre, mustard, and maroon. Inexpensive wooden pews face up to the altar, which is covered by a Moorish dome touted for its acoustics. From here, walk into the sacristy to the right; then upstairs to the "Father President's office" to gaze at the compound below. Next tour the convento, also attached to the church.

Concepcion, still an active parish church today, started out as a mission in 1716 in East Texas and was eventually moved to San Anto-

Concepcion church was built so well in about 1755 that it never crumbled into disarray.

nio in 1731. But its history after the mission period is even more vivid. Mexican revolutionaries holed up here, those Texas revolutionists we mentioned earlier fought nearby, the U.S. Army used it as a camp, and once it even was utilized as a cattle pen! In 1898 Teddy Roosevelt trained his Rough Riders nearby.

You can see the mission complex in as little as thirty minutes, if you don't linger. The facilities are minimal here; there are a few exhibits but as of this date, no slide shows or refreshment vending machines.

History

Concepcion has had what you might call a vagabond history, since it was one of the three missions moved to San Antonio in 1731 from East Texas. One of the first missions built by the Spanish among the Tejas tribes, Concepcion was established in 1716 near present-day Douglass in Nacogdoches County. But when the nearby protective presidio was shut down due to cost cutting, the missionaries requested that they be allowed to move the three missions to a safer area. The missions were moved in 1730 to a location in central Texas on the Colorado River. For some reason this site didn't work out, and the missions soon moved to the San Antonio River in 1731. Moving was no small feat. After all, the distance was about 375 miles and required carrying church furnishings across big rivers, not to mention the herding of all the cattle, horses, mules and burros.

Concepcion was set up on its present site, which is a little east of the San Antonio River and about two and a half miles from the Alamo, to serve the Coahuiltecan Indians. At its peak, the mission had some 250–300 Indians living there.

The stone church, finished in 1755 and made out of a limestone called tufa from a nearby quarry, was located in the southeastern portion of the walled-in square. These walls had Indian living quarters built into them, and these along with the granary, which extended southward from the present-day sacristy, no longer exist. Besides a convento attached to the church, there were also carpenter, blacksmith, and textile shops. An irrigation ditch, or acequia,

The simple beauty of the Concepcion chapel is shown in the intricate carved stonework on the church entrance.

flowed through the compound farther west of the church. Outside the enclosure was the mission farm where crops such as corn, beans, watermelons, and sweet potatoes were grown. Still further away was the mission ranch, which had its own brand.

In 1792, Concepcion was partially secularized, and some of its land distributed to the Indians. For a while it was a sub-mission of San Jose; then it was completely closed down in 1813.

About this time, a revolutionary army led by Mexican Bernardo Gutierrez headquartered here while it attacked local Spanish officials in an earlier aborted attempt to get Texas out from under Spanish rule.

Later on in October of 1835 came the so-called Battle of Concepcion, which came about when a volunteer army of Texans headed by Stephen F. Austin marched from Gonzales to capture San Antonio at the beginning of the Texas Revolution. There were several skirmishes in the area as the army waited on the fringe of town—one

The twin bell towers of Concepcion church give this mission its distinctive look.

of them a quarter of a mile from Concepcion led by Jim Bowie, James Fannin, and Juan Seguin. Eventually old Ben Milam took the forces into San Antonio and handily defeated General Cos. This defeat in turn led to General Santa Anna's return grudge fight at the Alamo.

In the 1840s Concepcion was used by the U.S. Army as a military camp, and John R. Bartlett, who visited the mission in 1850, described still another use: "The two towers and dome . . . make quite an imposing appearance when seen from a distance, but on approaching it, we found it not only desolated but desecrated, the church portion being used as an enclosure for cattle, the filth from which covered the floor . . . a foot or more."

Fortunately along came the Brothers of Mary, founders of St. Mary's School (now a local university), who occupied and restored the place from around 1859 to 1911. They restored the church and used the farm land to supply the school. And in the hot summer, faculty members even used it as a vacation spot for swimming and fishing. In more recent times, St. John's Seminary was built next door and a Catholic orphanage was established across Mission Road.

Architecture and Restoration

Concepcion's church originally had colorful geometric designs painted on its facade, though this effect is difficult to imagine now, with the rather austere greyish-white look that predominates the chapel. About the only remnants left

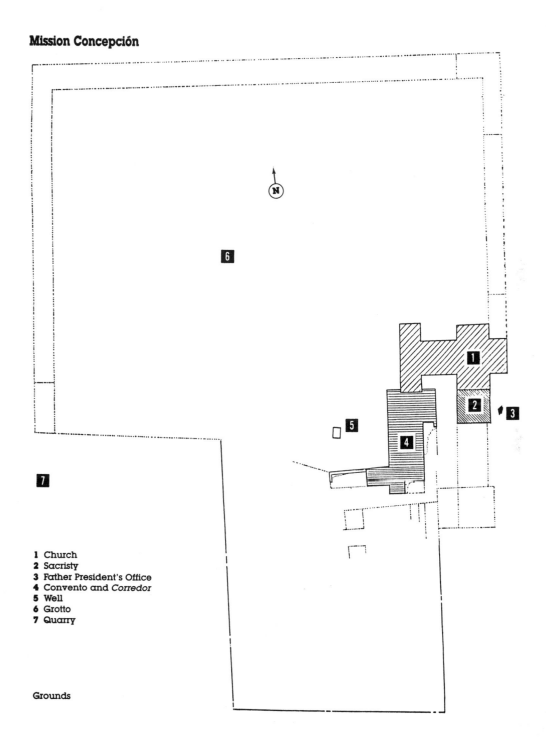

Mission Concepción

1 Church
2 Sacristy
3 Father President's Office
4 Convento and *Corredor*
5 Well
6 Grotto
7 Quarry

Grounds

of these frescoes can be seen inside in the confessional/belfry and convento.

The church, made of tufa, has twin towers and a Moorish dome. The tops of the towers are pyramidical with four lookout windows and a tiny iron cross on each. The entrance is the only really decorative part of Concepcion's architecture. Sculptured stonework frames large wooden doors. The design features a triangle above with a cross and shell-shaped recess in it. To the sides are half columns and flowered geometric designs.

Inside, the church is laid out in cruciform style (cross-shaped) with a vaulted ceiling. White walls are set off with accent colors of ochre, mustard, and maroon, and Spanish-type candle fixtures. At the rear is the usual transept and altar. The floor is flagstone, and the walls are four feet thick. The outside and inside facings of the walls are of cut stones, with the space in between filled with small stones and adobe.

To the left as you come in is the confessional room, or belfry (or St. Michael's Chapel). To the right is the baptistry. The baptismal font is of sculptured stone and used to be lined with copper. To the right rear of the sanctuary is the sacristy, or room for the priests' vestments, etc. Above it is what they call the "Father President's office," once used as a missionary administrative office. A small window looks down from it into the sanctuary.

To the right of the church and attached onto the front south tower is the convento. One of the rooms has the pale remains of that fresco called the "Eye of God," which peers down at you from the ceiling. No mischief for the friars here, they were being watched. The convento

The domed Concepcion church is well known for its acoustics.

has a roofed corridor that runs the length of the front with arched openings looking out on the patio and well.

As said before, comparatively little restoration has been done here at Concepcion. What has fallen into disarray, has been left there, and what has lasted, has been left alone. Of course, some minor restoration was done in the latter half of the 1800s by the Brothers of Mary and the Catholic Church to clean it up during the cattle pen era.

Directions to Mission Concepcion

If you're downtown in San Antonio, begin at the intersection of Market and South Alamo Street (the Alamo and HemisFair Plaza front this street). Go south on South Alamo, then turn left on St. Mary's, and just follow the Mission Trail signs. St. Mary's turns into Roosevelt, and after going under the underpass, turn right on Lone Star, and then go straight ahead on Mission Road. Stay on it until you reach the corner of Felisa and Mission Road, where Concepcion's parking lot is located.

If you are coming from somewhere else in the city, get on the Hwy 90 freeway and exit at Probandt; go south a couple of blocks and turn left on Mitchell. Then turn right on Mission Road. Concepcion is only two blocks down, where the road intersects Felisa.

Tours of Concepcion

The park service offers no guided tours for individuals as of this date. But pick up a self guided tour brochure at the park entrance. Several commercial bus tours stop at Concepcion on their mission tours, which embark from the Alamo daily.

Annual Events

Week of August 6
Semana de las Misiones—This is a week-long celebration at all San Antonio missions, with a different activity at one mission each day. The festivities always fall during the week of August 6. They usually include food booths, Mexican music and

The arched corridor on the convento building.

dance, religious services, speeches, and exhibits. Free admission.

Sunday in early August
Parish Festival—An all-day event, it has food booths, dancing, music, and games. Open to the public, the festival has free admission.

What to See Nearby

If you don't intend to follow the Mission Trail south to tour the other three missions, then you might like to take in another historic site, the Yturri-Edmunds Home and Mill, at 257 Yellowstone (534-8237). The mid-1800s adobe structure and grist mill is only about one-half mile north on Mission Road, where Yellowstone intersects. The San Antonio Conservation Society runs the home and offers guided tours and demonstrations. There is a small fee. Days and hours open may vary.

Mission San Juan

Mission San Juan Capistrano

9101 Graf, San Antonio/Museum/Open 9 a.m. to 6 p.m. daily/Free/(512) 532-5840

Historians are wont to disagree among themselves, but many think Mission San Juan is near the site on the San Antonio River where Spaniards first discovered and named the area in 1691.

"We found at this place the rancheria of the Indians of the Payaya tribe . . . I called this place San Antonio de Padua, because it was his feast day. In the language of the Indians, it is called Yanaguana . . . On this day, there were so many buffaloes that the horses stampeded . . .," wrote Fr. Damian Massanet, whose cohort on the expedition, Governor Don Domingo de Teran, also claims to have named the area.

Whoever takes the credit, the name for San Antonio, or Saint Anthony, stuck. Teran got the idea to put missions here.

"I discovered that they (the Indians) were docile and affectionate, were naturally friendly, and were decidedly agreeable to us. I saw the possibility of using them to form missions, the first on the Rio Grande, at the presidio, and another at this point," he wrote in his diary. Later friars would have the same idea. Thus San Antonio became a way station for the missions farther away in East Texas and eventually the capital of the Texas provincial territory.

Unlike Concepcion, San Juan still has its square, and it appears straight out of the eighteenth century, with its bucolic setting in an old, rather isolated part of town. It is third on the Mission Trail in south San Antonio, and quite endearing. Again, this is part of the San Antonio Missions National Historical Park.

The charm of San Juan lies not in any stately architecture but in its simplicity. It is in fact a very plain mission. The church is even stark, with only the bell tower wall to give it any religious character. But because it is surrounded by trees and foliage and few houses in this sparsely settled area, the quaint aura of the eighteenth century is inescapable when you enter the square from the arched southwest entrance. The courtyard within the square (which actually isn't a square but an odd-shaped rectangle) is lined with green grass and clover. The church (still in use), convento, and ruins of the hospederia (guest room) and Indian quarters help form the walls of the mission compound.

San Juan (short for Mission San Juan Capistrano) is one of the three missions, along with Concepcion and Espada, which relocated to San Antonio from East Texas in 1731.

After first obtaining the self-guided tour brochure at the park entrance, simply follow the plaques around the square. You can easily view it in 30 minutes, but I suggest you tarry longer at the last stop, the restored convento-museum. It is small, but it is one of the better mission museums. It has some excellent exhibits about archeological digs and the Coahuiltecan Indians. Actually only two buildings are currently open to the public, the church and convento museum. The rest are remnants of walls or off-limits restored residences used by church or park officials.

The grassy areas outside the square are fine for picnicking, and parks are only blocks away. No fast food franchises are close by. But then if there were, the rustic appeal of the place would vanish.

History

San Juan not only started out in another place, East Texas, it started out with another name: San Jose de los Nazonis. But since there was already a mission by the name of San Jose when it moved to San Antonio in 1731, the title was changed. Mission San Juan Capistrano means mission of St. John Capistran. St. John was a roving Franciscan preacher who became famous for leading a Christian army in a victory against the Turks in 1456.

The mission first started out in 1716 near present Cushing, not far from Nacogdoches. Meant to serve the Nazoni Indians, it was soon abandoned by Spain in 1719 when the French became hostile. Spain returned in 1721 to reestablish it, but soon cost cutting caused the nearby presidio to close down. The three mis-

This pastoral setting will greet you at San Juan.

sions (Concepcion and Espada were the other two), without their protection, requested to be moved elsewhere. First they tried a spot on the Colorado River in 1730, but this didn't work out either. Soon they all ended up in San Antonio, bag and baggage hauled tediously by cart from East Texas.

The mission began with only crude mud huts on its present spot on the east bank of the San Antonio River, south of Mission San Jose and about seven miles from downtown San Antonio.

But by about 1745, modest stone buildings had been erected for a friary and a granary. And by 1756, a church, whose foundations can still be seen near the present restrooms, was built. Some 265 Indians lived in the compound around this time. The remnants of the square today reflect its appearance in the 1780s, with Indian quarters on the north and west walls.

Two missionaries along with several Spanish soldiers with swivel guns to ward off the Apaches minded the store. The standard mission carpenter, blacksmith, and textile shops flourished, and crops of corn, melons, beans, chile, and cotton sprouted in the nearby farm fields. San Juan's ranch, Rancho de la Mora (also on the San Antonio River, somewhere south of present-day Floresville) provided meat and wool. Once a week cattle were driven from there, slaughtered, and given to the Indians.

Sometime in the 1760s when the Indian population was high and the mission thriving, a newer and larger church was begun on the east side of the square. It was never finished, and the ruins can still be seen today. San Juan was partially secularized, along with the other missions, in 1792. It became a sort of sub-mission, overseen by the Espada missionary. The present church, which was originally a granary, came into use sometime after 1800.

In 1824 San Juan was completely de-missionized, although Spanish and Indian families continued to live in the area. The old stone and adobe house on the edge of the east wall is from this post-colonial period.

Though San Juan deteriorated over the years, it doesn't seem to have been subject to the destruction the other missions experienced. They were used as cattle pens and stomping grounds for rambunctious soldiers. San Juan continued to be an active, viable community. The church's roof fell in but was repaired in 1909, and since

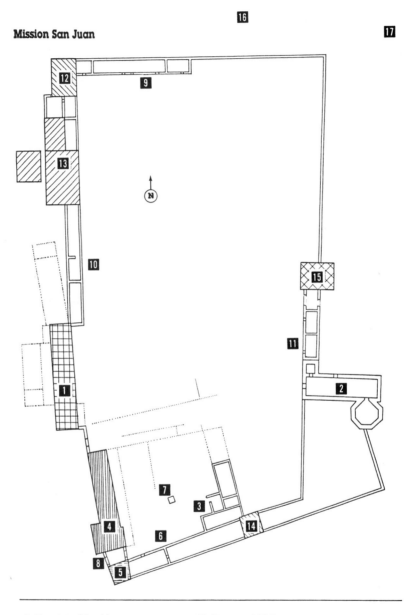

Mission San Juan

1 Church and Sacristy
2 Late Colonial Church Ruins
3 Early Colonial Church Ruins
4 Convento
5 *Hospederia*
6 Ruins of Convento Workrooms
7 Well
8 *Porteria*
9 North Wall Indian
Quarters Ruins
10 West Wall Indian
Quarters Ruins

11 Compound Walls
and Wall Ruins
12 Meeting and Storage Room
13 Office and Rectory
14 Post-Colonial House
Ruins Converted
to Restrooms
15 Post-Colonial House
16 Well North of Compound
17 Lillian Daura House

These gabled buildings on the edge of the mission square are actually reproductions, but fit into the centuries-aged ambiance.

then it has been regularly used as a parish church.

Architecture and Restoration

As mentioned, San Juan's church is outwardly unadorned, but still has a certain primitive grace to it. Even the visiting Fr. Morfi remarked of San Juan in 1777, "The church is neat and in good order, though it does not compare with those described (Alamo, Concepcion, and San Jose)." Though his comment probably referred to an earlier church here, it shows that San Juan was much less grand than the other missions.

The wood door entrance, of the rectangular stone church appears to be an afterthought, it is so small. The one identifying characteristic is the Spanish bell tower at the end, which makes for an interesting silhouette against the sky with the three bells and a tiny iron cross at the top. Surprisingly, the lack of rococo on the church and the quaintness of the buildings in the square make the mission an excellent unspoiled photo subject.

Inside the church is just as modest. It simply doesn't have the grace of the other mission chapels. There is no domed ceiling—just a flat one with rafters. The room is a rectangle, narrower than it is tall, and the walls are painted white. Cheap wooden pews and a simple altar (though there are gilded statues) indicate that a poor parish worships here.

Apparently at one time, crude, colorful frescoes lined the inside walls, depicting musicians playing instruments. When asked about them in the late 1880s, local priest Father Bouchu explained, "They were probably permitted to satisfy the Indian nature's love of color."

Around 1967, restoration began on the church and convento. Two old-looking houses with gabled roofs were built atop the foundation ruins of the Indian homes and nineteenth-century dwellings on the northern part of the west wall. To the novice they look old, except for the shingle roofs.

Museum and Archeology

History got buried literally at San Juan. During restoration work begun in 1967, archeological excavations uncovered some graves in both foundations of the churches, plus innumerable artifacts in other areas.

Slides and explanations of what was found can be seen in the small museum in the restored convento next to the mission entrance. The artifacts themselves, such as arrowheads, bone tools, pottery sherds, and coins are also attractively displayed.

The skeletons (not on display) from the east church ruins date from the 1760s to 1790s, and archeologists were thus able to make some observations about the Coahuiltecan Indians: "The average male was 5.7 feet tall, and the average female 5.4 feet . . . The pathology study of their bones revealed the diseases they suffered: arthritis, osteoporosis, osteitis, paget's disease, and syphilis." The Indians seemed to be plagued with some of the same diseases that

The starkly simple San Juan church has only one religious characteristic, its triangular shaped three-bell tower. No wonder, it started out as a granary.

The grassy expanse of San Juan's compound exudes peace and quiet.

still plague us. Excavations also turned up the fact that underneath the present church was an old foundation that probably served as an earlier granary.

This is a small museum, but the exhibits are well done for mission history enthusiasts, and the kids will enjoy the Indian artifacts. Besides the archeology and Coahuiltecan displays, other displays include data on the building of San Juan, the establishment of San Antonio missions, presidios, the economy of the missions, secularization, and the Franciscans.

Directions to San Juan

If coming from downtown to see this mission only, take IH 37 south, then exit on S.E. Military Drive going west. Take a left on South Presa, and later a right on Graf which will take you a few blocks to the mission. You can see the bell tower; just follow the signs to the parking lot and entrance.

However, if you've been on the Mission Trail visiting the other missions, you have just been to San Jose. As you come out of the San Jose parking lot, turn left on Mission Road, and just follow the Mission Trail signs to San Juan. In other words, San Juan is further south of San Jose.

Tours of San Juan

The National Park Service doesn't normally give guided tours to individuals, but pick up the self-guided tour brochure at the entrance, and proceed around the square.

Local commercial bus companies do give tours of the missions.

Annual Events

In late May, the Sunday of Memorial weekend
Parish Festival—This is an all-day event, beginning with outdoor Mass. Open to the public, it includes food (with the accent on Mexican) booths, games, music, and entertainment. Free admission.

Week of August 6
Semana de las Misiones—One event is always held at San Juan during the Week of the Missions, which includes special festivities at the various missions on different days. The week features religious services, festivals, music, speeches and exhibits. Free admission.

Espada's rustic chapel also boasts a three-bell wall tower.

Mission Espada

Mission San Francisco de la Espada

10040 Espada Road, San Antonio/Open 9 a.m. to 6 p.m. daily/Free/(512) 627-2021

Much like a lonely stepchild, Mission Espada languishes on the southern fringe of San Antonio as the furthest away of the city's missions. The setting looms pastoral, because it *is*. Farmland and a few small houses surround the mission much like they did centuries ago, despite the fact that the mission lies just south of busy Loop 410.

Espada is a homely mission, but therein lies its simple charm. Much of it is in foundation ruins and unrestored, except for the convento and the endearing rustic chapel with its bell tower. Interestingly enough, Mission San Francisco de la Espada has a longer history than the other San Antonio missions, because it was the original San Francisco de los Tejas, the first mission established in East Texas by the Spanish in 1690. It was abandoned and moved to several locations because of French threats and hostile

Indians before it ended up in San Antonio in 1731 with a slight name change.

Strangely, while part of the mission itself fell into ruins, Espada's irrigation system still stands today, miraculously watering the same fields it did hundreds of years ago. In fact, it's probably the oldest acequia system still working in the United States, with the only Spanish aqueduct left standing. The aqueduct, which can be seen on the way to or from Espada, ingeniously carries water from the dam on the San Antonio River across Piedras Creek to the mission and the lands below.

If you're taking in all of the missions on the Mission Trail, it's probably best to see the aqueduct on the way from San Juan to Espada. Aqueduct Park is located just off Espada Road and roughly one and a half miles farther south is Espada Mission itself.

There isn't a great deal to see at Espada, in terms of touring the structures, since only the chapel and information center are actually open to the public. But the National Park Service is currently doing some restoration work. You can still view the foundation ruins and get the lay of the compound. These compound walls are shaped in a slightly irregular square.

You park on the south side of the mission and enter through an opening in the south wall. To the right in the southeast corner is the information center (also a combination community center for older citizens). On that same corner is an object worth studying, the corner bastion. Similar to the restored one at San Jose, this is the only surviving bastion left in tact in the local missions. A squat, round, rock fortification, it contains holes for cannons and muskets to defend the adjacent walls.

Out here at Espada you can feel what it was like to be isolated in a remote mission. Being the farthest away, it was particularly preyed on by the Apache Indians. Though the compound itself was defensible, Apaches would steal horses and swoop down on individuals straying from the complex. One day in the 1730s five mission Indian women and two boys went out to gather fruit. The boys ended up captured and the hapless women murdered.

Likewise, you can imagine Espada Mission as a likely camp for the Texan army during the Texas Revolution. Although historians disagree on which Texas patriots actually used Espada, it is likely Espada played some part. One local tradition has Stephen F. Austin camping here with the newly organized volunteer army when it first came up from Gonzales to catch General Cos at San Antonio. Other versions have James Bowie and James Fannin making it their headquarters and fighting off a band of Mexican soldiers.

Make the rounds of the square with brochure in hand to see the outline of the various foundation ruins, including the granary, the unfinished church, and the Indian quarters. The convento has been restored, but is closed to the public since it is used as a rectory. Espada, like the other San Antonio missions, is a thriving parish church. The chapel itself is certainly nothing grand like San Jose's or Concepcion's, but nevertheless it is appealing in its simplicity and warm intimacy.

Before leaving Espada, the stouthearted should walk the few rustic trails wandering outside the walls towards the river. Anywhere outside the compound is suitable for picnicking, provided you have your own "vittles." Don't expect any fast food shops nearby. There is peace and tranquility here, disturbed only by an occasional hum of a single-engine plane from Stinson Field.

The Espada Aqueduct and San Antonio's Unique Early Water System

Watering crops wasn't so easy in mission times when you consider there was no modern irrigation, much less a water system.

That's why the Spanish shrewdly built the missions near the San Antonio River. There was still the problem of getting water from the river to the fields, and thus a unique acequia (canal or ditch) system was created along the river for the various mission farms. Today you can still view remnants of this open canal system in

One of the few walls remaining of Espada's square frames the chapel.

Probably the oldest acequia system in the nation can be found in San Antonio. This ancient Espada Aqueduct at nearby Aqueduct Park is still transporting water to fields below.

parts of the city, which continued to use it up until the 1870s. The Espada Aqueduct remains in use as a salute to the Spanish friars' ingenuity.

The crude beginnings of this unusual water system started first around 1719 with the Acequia Madre, or "Mother Ditch" (the Alamo Ditch), designed to irrigate fields for Mission San Antonio de Valero.

The Acequia San Jose is thought to have been completed around 1730, and the Concepcion, San Juan, and Espada canals begun in 1731. Then finally a canal system (Acequia San Pedro) that brought water from San Pedro Springs was started for the townfolk and presidio in 1738.

The Espada acequia system posed more problems than the others. Water had to be brought from the Espada dam about two miles north on the San Antonio River *across* Piedras Creek. For this reason the arched stone aqueduct was built to carry water across the creek bed to the Espada fields below. The aged, vine-covered structure still sends water down the trough today to water the rural fields near Espada.

You can scrutinize the aqueduct in Aqueduct Park, which is approximately one and a half miles north of Espada Mission by road. It is just off Espada Road. There is a small, clean area for picnicking right by the aqueduct as it passes over the tiny Piedras Creek. And there are plenty of rustic hiking trails on the hill above the aqueduct. They are guaranteed to burn up kiddie energy.

The Espada dam and canal system are thought to have been started in 1731, but the aqueduct itself was not completed until 1735–1740. The 270-foot dam is another unusual engineering feat. After hundreds of years, it still stands, with the layers of brush, gravel, and rocks cemented together over time by the lime salts in the water. For years people thought the dam curved the wrong way, but that is because only one corner of a box dam shows. The other corner is under the surface. Only recently National Park Service researchers discovered that the San Juan dam still stands! It was hidden in a dry bed of the river cut off by rechanneling.

The Espada Ditch Company did some patch-repair work on the system in 1895. In 1941, the San Antonio Conservation Society bought up land adjacent to the aqueduct, and the aqueduct was declared a national historic landmark in 1965.

Want to know more about San Antonio's historic water system? Check the exhibits in the small San Antonio Water Museum, run by the San Antonio City Water Board in an old (1868) renovated house at 1000 East Commerce. But be sure to call first, to make an appointment on weekdays. The phone is 225-7461.

History

Keeping up with Espada's elusive history is like following a soap opera heroine who keeps remarrying and changing her name. As said earlier, the mission was first established as San Francisco de los Tejas in East Texas in 1690 when the Spanish wanted to stake out their claim in Texas. They disliked France encroaching on their territory. When the ill-fated La Salle had wandered across Texas, Spain stepped up its mission activity. An expedition of Alonso de Leon and Fr. Damian Massanet founded a mission on San Pedro Creek near present-day Weches to ostensibly serve the area's Indians, whom they called the Tejas.

Epidemics and hostile Indians led the missionaries to abandon San Francisco three years later. The friars actually burned it down themselves. A log mission replica is now located in the vicinity of this former site at Mission Tejas State Historical Park (see later section for more details).

It wasn't until some years later in 1716 that Spain decided to reoccupy East Texas and start up even more missions. One of the six begun was the reincarnation of San Francisco at a site ten miles farther east from its first location. The new site was on the Neches River, near present-day Alto. This time the mission was called Nuestro Padre San Francisco de los Tejas, and the missionary life was still tough sledding.

The French drove the Spanish missionaries out in another three years, and the mission had to be reestablished again in 1721, apparently at the same site. This time it was called San Francisco de los Neches (supposedly for the Neche Indians). Spanish economizing closed down the nearby protective presidio and sent San Francisco and two other missions (Concepcion and San Juan, then called San Jose de los Nazonis) packing once again. After locating briefly on a Colorado River site, all the missions finally landed in 1731 at San Antonio where San Francisco was renamed for the last time as Mission San Francisco de la Espada. This means mission of St. Francis of La Espada. Espada is the word for sword, but no one seems to know why this word is in the name, unless it honored some prominent person's name. Whatever, the mission has come to be known simply as "Espada."

A stone friary was finished in 1745, and the small church by 1756. Even before that, somewhere between 1735 and 1740, Espada's famous aqueduct was completed. A larger church was begun by 1762 near the south square wall. But the quality control proved poor, and eventually the completed building had to be torn down. Indian quarters were located in the square walls. Espada's ranch, Rancho de las Cabras, was located some miles away on the San Antonio River near Floresville.

The peak Indian population was probably around 200. A Father Garcia, stationed here in 1760, wrote a guide on the Coahuiltecan language used by the various Indian tribes and included a few interesting observations of their habits, such as their penchant for eating the narcotic buds of the cactus peyotl and making liquor from the mountain-laurel bean.

Espada was partially secularized in 1792 and completely so in 1824. In 1826, a company of Mexican dragoons was stationed here to protect settlers, and in 1835, as mentioned earlier, Texas revolutionaries probably camped and fought here.

The place fell mostly into ruins after this, until along came a guardian angel in the form of Father Francis Bouchu. Bouchu both lived and worked here and almost single-handedly rebuilt the original little chapel himself. He first came to San Antonio as assistant pastor at San Fernando Church, but fell in love with the old Espada mission and ministered to the parishioners there from 1858 to 1909. A jack-of-all-trades, he also cranked out on his own little printing press a Spanish language catechism, which came to be used in several dioceses. Ever since Bouchu's era, Espada has served as a parish church, and for a while it served as a parochial school.

Architecture and Restoration

The dominant feature of this mission is naturally the little stone chapel built by 1756. It is by no means a grandiose structure but simply a rudimentary pastoral church, with its only significant feature being the appealing three-bell tower on the front wall.

Mission Espada

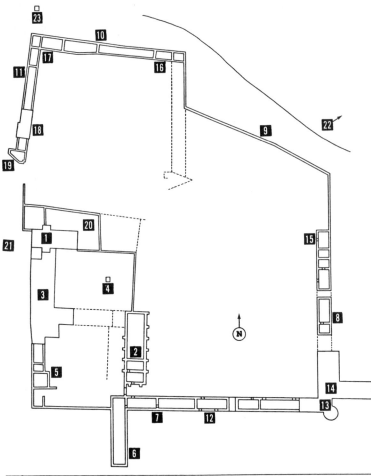

1 Church and Sacristy
2 Walls of Granary and Late Colonial Church
3 Convento Converted to Rectory and Office
4 Convento Well
5 Workshop Walls
6 Walls of the Late Colonial Granary
7 Indian Quarters, South Wall of Compound
8 Indian Quarters, East Wall of Compound
9 Northeast Wall
10 Indian Quarters, North Wall of Compound
11 Indian Quarters, West Wall of Compound
12 Chavagneux House Ruins
13 Bastion and Adjoining Rooms
14 Old Schoolhouse
15 Oaks House and Convent Ruins
16 Conti House Ruins
17 Cuellar House Ruins
18 Old Classroom
19 Walls Associated with Gateway
20 Camposanto
21 Sluice Gate
22 Kilns
23 Well Northwest of Compound

The only bit of slight embellishment on the entire building is at the entrance where a sculptured stone Moorish arch frames the carved wooden doors. Actually, this small chapel was probably initially intended to be just the sacristy of a much larger church that never got built.

On the left of the church's front is a crude, wooden cross, which has a long tale behind it. Local legend says that about 1870 the congregation carried it about the compound praying for rain, and lo and behold, torrents fell. So Father Bouchu placed it there to remind them of the power of prayer. However, recent research shows the cross didn't appear until around 1936.

Inside, the small chapel is shaped in a cross, with a red tile floor and a flat ceiling of rough-hewn beams. White walls and wooden pews face a simple altar with fresh flowers, lighted candles, and three carved wooden statues. The main one, of St. Francis, is thought to be original with the church. The other two are of Mary and Jesus.

Don't overlook the well to the left of the chapel and in front of the arched convento. It has wrought iron grillwork on the top similar to the one at Concepcion.

As for Espada restoration, it began around 1870 with Father Bouchu's one-man job of dedicated renovation. When he arrived, only the rear wall and facade of the chapel were standing. He rebuilt the side walls on old foundations and added a roof. Author William Corner, who wrote of the padre in 1890, called him a "priest, lawyer, bricklayer, stone mason, photographer, historian, printer . . . He is simple, unaffected, and garrulous, and meets the wants of the little settlement."

Further restoration has been done since 1909 in piecemeal fashion by the Catholic Church, and currently, the National Park Service is doing some.

Directions to Mission Espada

If you come from downtown to see just Mission Espada alone (and don't take the Mission Trail tour of all four), take IH 37 south. Espada is on the southern edge of San Antonio. Turn

The Moorish arch framing the doors is the only decorative stonework at the quaint, diminutive chapel at Espada.

An original fortified corner bastion still survives in the wall ruins of Espada's square.

right or west onto Loop 410 and drive for almost four miles, until you exit at Roosevelt Avenue, where you turn left under the freeway going south for just one block. There take a left on Chavaneaux Road and go east for almost two miles. Espada will be on your left. (Before you get there, Chavaneaux runs into Espada Road at a "Y", but you just keep on driving straight, bearing slightly to the right.) When you sight Espada, don't turn in the first road into it. Wait and turn left onto Camino Coahuilteca Street. The parking lot will be on your left, and you enter the mission park at a gate in the south square wall. The information center is at the southeast corner of the mission compound.

If you tour all four missions on the Mission Trail, you will be coming from Mission San Juan. There are two routes from San Juan. The blue and white Mission Trail signs lead you to the right from San Juan onto Villa Main. But since there is a low water crossing on this route, the National Park Service usually recommends taking a left on Ashley Road (going west). There will be signs directing you where to turn off of Ashley onto Espada Road, which takes you to Espada Mission, approximately two miles further south. Besides, on this route you can stop by Espada Aqueduct at Aqueduct Park, which is just off Espada Road, on the way to the mission.

Tours

No guided tours for individuals are provided here yet. Just get a brochure at the information center, and follow the map and recommended self-guided tour.

Commercial bus tours of the missions leave daily from in front of the Alamo in downtown San Antonio.

Annual Events

Week of August 6

Semana de las Misiones—One special event is always held at Espada during the Week of the Missions. Each mission participates, and activities include festivals, music, religious services, talks, and exhibits. Free admission.

Sunday in early October

Parish Festival—This is usually held on the Sunday of the first weekend in October. It begins around 11 a.m. and lasts all day and features live music, games, and food booths. Admission is free.

Goliad Mission and Presidio

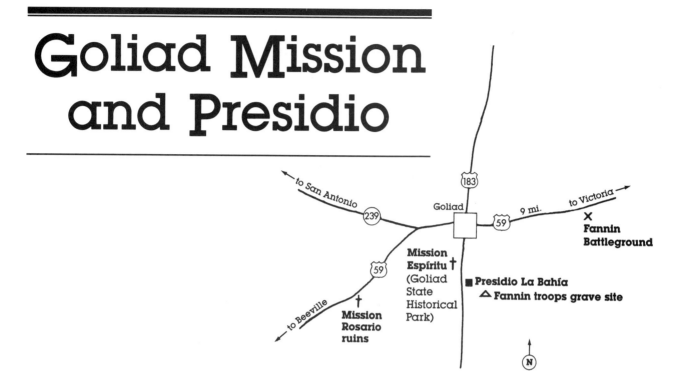

Goliad is a pleasurable surprise in the litany of small Texas towns. It's chock full of historic battlegrounds and grave sites and even has a bonafide "hanging tree." It is Texas history in the flesh, right up there along side San Antonio and San Jacinto. So you might as well take a detour from San Antonio down to Goliad, only about 95 miles to the southeast, to relive the Texas revolutionary saga.

Investigate Mission Espiritu and Presidio La Bahia, the site of the Goliad Massacre, where Colonel James Fannin and about 351 of his men were executed by the Mexicans only a few weeks after the disastrous fall of the Alamo. This is the next chapter in the story of Texas independence, which fostered another battlecry shouted at San Jacinto—"Remember Goliad."

Goliad embraces a rare combination of a restored mission and presidio, all in one vicinity, as they were traditionally set up by the Spanish in the 1700s. The mission was designed to prose-lytize the native Indians and the presidio to fend off those who didn't want to be prose-lytized and other hostile forces, like the French.

This is the only mission-presidio duo in tact we know of in Texas. For instance, the presidio in San Antonio is long gone, and only the chapel of San Elizario Presidio remains in El Paso.

Picnic/Camping Available at State Park

Both Mission Espiritu Santo and La Bahia Presidio are located just south of Goliad on Hwy 183. And conveniently, Espiritu Santo is actually part of Goliad State Historical Park, which has excellent, clean facilities for camping and picnicking. Besides screen shelters and RV hookups, there is a pool and boating and fishing on the San Antonio River. See a ten-minute slide show and exhibit on Texas missions at the park headquarters.

Special Days at Mission and Presidio

Look for two annual events. One on May 5 when an outside Mass celebrates the national Mexican holiday, Cinco de Mayo, at Presidio La Bahia. This is held just outside the southwest corner of the fort, near the birthplace of General Ignacio Zaragoza, whose father was stationed at the fort. General Zaragoza was a hero of the Mexican battle this holiday commemorates. The other special event falls on or near December 12, when Mission Espiritu Santo holds its Feast of the Virgin of Guadalupe Candlelight Mass. This evening Mass, which also features luminarias lighting up the road to the mission, approximates historical services held for the Indians.

What to See Elsewhere in Goliad

Goliad is resplendent with historical markers. The aforesaid Zaragoza birthplace is just outside La Bahia's walls, and the Fannin Memorial, where the massacred troops were buried, is just one-quarter mile away. The site of the Battle of Coleto Creek, or Fannin Battleground State Historic Site, is nine miles east of Goliad on Hwy 59. Don't overlook the 1894 courthouse and its hanging tree on the town square either.

Incidentally, there was another mission, Rosario, built in the Goliad area in 1754. But only ruins are left and they were covered with brush as of this writing; so I don't recommend taking time to see the site unless you're a die-hard historian. The ruins are located about six miles west of Goliad on Hwy 59. (See "Miscellaneous Missions")

Goliad County Chamber of Commerce
Box 606
Goliad, Texas 77963 (512) 645-3563

Goliad State Historical Park
P.O. Box 727
Goliad, Texas 77963

Presidio La Bahia
Box 57
Goliad, Texas 77963

Mission Espiritu Santo

Mission Espiritu Santo de Zuniga

On Hwy 183, about one-quarter mile south of Goliad in Goliad State Historical Park/Museum, camping, and recreational facilities/ Open 8 a.m. to 12 noon and 1 p.m. to 5 p.m. daily/Park entrance fee ($2 per car) serves as admission/(512) 645-3405

Mission Espiritu Santo has a lot going for it that makes it novel among Texas missions. To begin with, it's situated in the middle of a state park with recreational and camping facilities, so that you can combine a campout with a tour of a historical mission. In fact, the very reason for Goliad State Historical Park's being is the mission.

Espiritu Santo has been handsomely restored and a museum and slide shows added. There are weaving and pottery demonstrations plus a nature trail that shows how the Aranama Indians utilized native plants for survival. In all, the activities are varied enough to keep the whole family sufficiently entertained.

Another unusual aspect about Espiritu Santo is the importance it played in Texas' ultimate industry, cattle. Many of the missions had cattle ranches all their own, because the Spaniards were seasoned cattlemen and brought the herds along with them. But Espiritu had the largest ranch of all. It stretched roughly between Goliad and San Antonio and had an estimated 40,000 head!

Like the presidio down the road, the mission started out on the Texas coast at the site of La Salle's defunct colony. (The presidio was founded in 1721, the mission in 1722.) The two, which became known as the La Bahia mission and presidio, moved again in tandem and ended up in 1749 on the San Antonio River at what is now Goliad. Here the mission ministered mainly to the Aranama Indians, who proved more amenable to mission life than had the Karankawas.

To get to Espiritu, stop at the park headquarters and get a car permit ($2 per day), which allows the whole family to then peruse the mis-

High on a hill near Goliad sits the magnificent restored church of Espiritu Santo.

sion. It is just behind the headquarters and up a grassy hill. The whole park is neatly kept, the mission in particular. It's an inspiring sight to view Espiritu's romantic colonial structure standing out in the rural countryside.

The park staff will give you a park map, which has a more detailed map of the mission on the back. From there stroll up the walk to Espiritu. (But beware, as of this writing, fire ants were plentiful in the grass outside the walkway.) Head first for the museum, which is just left of the church entrance and in the old granary. Here attendants will be glad to answer questions and give a guided tour, unless it is too crowded. During the week in the school year, attendance is slow. But in summertime and on weekends it picks up.

What is there to see? Begin with the church. Its elegant facade is well proportioned and very pleasing to the eye. Sculptured stone work encloses the wooden door entrance and to the right is a covered octangular bell tower with a

cross on top. A few Moorish points or teeth stick up at the rear roof edge, much like they do at Mission Concepcion in San Antonio.

The church, the granary (where the museum is) and mission school workshop behind them are the limits of what can be physically toured inside. The rest of the mission grounds are simply low ruin walls or foundations that can be quickly viewed by glancing and walking around the square compound.

If you still feel like more walking, take the nature trail that starts just outside the northwest corner of the mission square. It's only about one-third of a mile. But first be sure to get that free brochure explaining the plants and how the Aranama Indians used them.

What about the park's other facilities? Besides screened shelters, tent sites, and hookups for trailers and RV's, it has a group shelter, swimming pool, picnic tables, and hiking trails. You can also fish or boat on the San Antonio River.

The Texas Ranching Business Gets its Start

This is where the Texas cattle business had its rudimentary beginnings. Well, perhaps it didn't just begin here in Goliad, but the whole area between Goliad and San Antonio was very instrumental in developing ranching. A lot of San Antonio missions had their ranches south of the city around Pleasanton and Floresville. And Mission Espiritu Santo's ranch was the biggest of all, extending roughly between the San Antonio and Guadalupe Rivers, almost as far north as San Antonio and Gonzales. See a map of it in the mission museum.

At its peak, Espiritu Santo had an estimated 40,000 head of cattle, not to mention a number of horses, mules, sheep, and goats. But cattle was the coin of the realm for the missions. Here at Espiritu, not only did the missionaries utilize the meat and leather, but they bartered hides and tallow for goods in San Antonio, the Rio Grande missions, and Saltillo.

Mission Indians were the ones who did the dusty, dirty work on this vast spread. They got on-the-job vaquero training whether they wanted it or not, because the two or three missionaries couldn't handle all the rough work plus their other duties. Most of the time the herds roamed on these huge grazing lands un-branded. But sporadic attempts were made in the fall to round them up.

History

Mission Nuestra Senora del Espiritu Santo de Zuniga was founded originally in 1722 on the Texas coast near present-day Lavaca Bay, on Garcitas Creek in Victoria County.

The mission's long name has a tale behind it. It means Our Lady of the Holy Spirit of Zuniga, and was partly derived from the Spaniard's original name for the great bay there: La Bahia del Espiritu Santo. Today, only a small inlet retains this title. The Zuniga part honors some then-illustrious viceroy of New Spain. Later the mission and presidio were popularly called La Bahia, even after they moved to the present site.

The mission-presidio complex was founded by the Aguayo expedition to discourage the French. That's why the exact spot of La Salle's failed colony was picked for its location. However, the Karankawa Indians proved cantankerous, and the mission and presidio had to move in 1726 to a spot on the Guadalupe River (at present-day Mission Valley, just north of Victoria).

Operations went smoothly here apparently, but the Spanish administration decided it

Note the Moorish points or teeth at the roof edge in this back view of Espiritu Santo church.

Remnants of original walls of this granary, which now houses the museum, can be seen at the right.

needed a fortified settlement to guard the main roads from Mexico to San Antonio and East Texas and the Texas port at Copano Bay. Thus, mission and presidio were ordered to move to their present location at Goliad on the San Antonio River in 1749.

The local Aranama Indians seemed to take to mission life at Espiritu Santo, and at one time the mission housed as many as 300 Indians. Of course, the Indians were sly at adopting only what *they* wanted to of this new civilization cast upon them.

"To withdraw them from their pagan dances and diabolical mitotes," writes a visiting Franciscan bigwig, Fr. Solis, in 1768, "the ministers have introduced some Spanish dances. These dances have been taught with violin and guitar accompaniment, and the Indians have learned them very well. For such performances they wear a special dress . . . and very gaudy, and use palms, crowns, masks and ayacastles. As a result they have partly forgotten their mitotes and pagan dances. I say partly, because when the ministers are not watching them they go off to the woods, and there hold their dances. . . ."

Espiritu's first structures were made of wood and adobe, but gradually stone buildings replaced them, and by 1777 a new church was dedicated.

Unlike most of the missions, Espiritu couldn't seem to get an irrigation system going for some reason and lost some of its crops in dry seasons. Perhaps the San Antonio River was too low in its banks at this point.

As the mission system declined, Espiritu closed later than the rest, in 1830. But prior to this, the whole place had begun to deteriorate. In 1812, for instance, the Spanish forces added to the mission's wear and tear by headquartering at Espiritu while fighting the Gutierrez-Magee Mexican revolutionists that took over nearby La Bahia presidio. One little skirmish nearby was called "The Battle of the White Cow" because it all started when an insurgent tried to corral a cow outside of the fort.

In later years, from around 1848 to the Civil War, the mission grounds were used first by the Hillyer Female Institute and later the Presbyterian's Aranama College for men. At one time, the people of Goliad generally referred to the mission as the "Aranama Mission" until more recent years when the original name has been reapplied. So don't be confused by the seemingly different names.

By the time the mission's land was deeded to the state and made into a state historical park in 1931, most of the mission was in ruins. Much restoration work was done in the 1930s, and

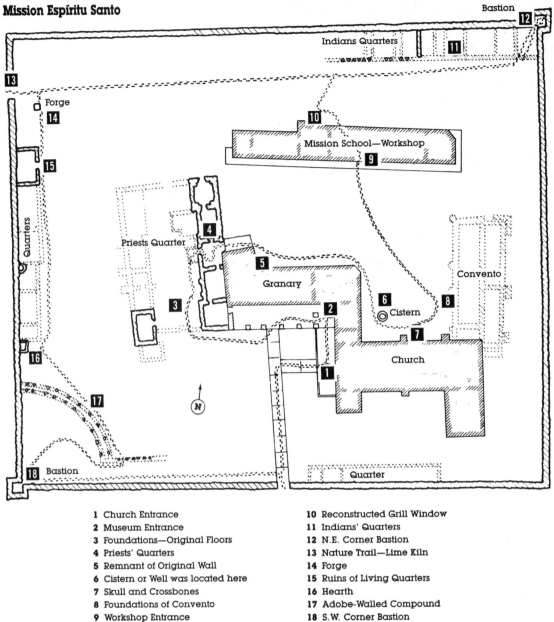

1 Church Entrance
2 Museum Entrance
3 Foundations—Original Floors
4 Priests' Quarters
5 Remnant of Original Wall
6 Cistern or Well was located here
7 Skull and Crossbones
8 Foundations of Convento
9 Workshop Entrance

10 Reconstructed Grill Window
11 Indians' Quarters
12 N.E. Corner Bastion
13 Nature Trail—Lime Kiln
14 Forge
15 Ruins of Living Quarters
16 Hearth
17 Adobe-Walled Compound
18 S.W. Corner Bastion

then more in the 1970s. The Texas Parks and Wildlife Department now maintains Espíritu.

Archeological Digs and Restoration

Very little of the Espíritu Santo compound was left by the 1930s when it became a state historical park. Only a small room on the north side of the granary (now where the museum slide show is) was still standing. The rest of the structures were much like the ruins of the old priests' quarters you see on the west side of the granary, and some were worse. But Humpty

Dumpty *was* put back together again, this time using the Civilian Conservation Corps. The granary, church, and workshop were rebuilt, and the surrounding square walls partially restored and stabilized.

Before and during all this, extensive archeological digs uncovered artifacts and foundations. Among the artifacts upturned were tools, door ornaments, arrowheads, brass objects, nails, spurs, horse bits, beads, and pottery sherds. All are on display in the museum. Archeologists discovered that there had been a well on the north side of the church near where

The skull and crossbones (symbolizing transitory life) was a typical mission motif.

History, restoration, archeological excavations, Indians, ranching, agriculture, mission life, and defense are some of the topics covered. There is an old census of the mission, an elaborately carved brass cannon from Presidio La Bahia, and an almost life-size replica of two men manning a corner bastion. An eight-and-a-half minute color slide show about the Coahuiltecan Indians can also be activated by punching a button.

The Mission Workshop building, behind the church and granary, serves as a "living" exhibit offering regular weaving and spinning demonstrations. Too, there are occasional pottery firings, using local clay. All this is designed to portray how the Indians learned eighteenth-century crafts at the mission. In the same building is a reproduction of the office of a *mayordomo*, the Indian convert appointed as overseer for the workshop.

it connects to the granary. And they also found remnants of foundations for a convento, probably never completed, attached to the church's north side also.

Museum and Mission Workshop Exhibits

This is one of the better mission museums, with appealing and well-designed displays. Housed in what was the granary, it begins with a large model of the mission compound in the late 1700s.

Exhibits highlight artifacts gathered in archeological digs, plus photos, documents, and maps.

Directions to Espiritu Santo

From the intersection of Hwys 183 and 59 in Goliad, take Hwy 183 south about one-quarter mile. Goliad State Historical Park's entrance is on the right, and the headquarters office is just off the road. Park there and get a car permit. Mission Espiritu Santo is not far behind, just a walk up the hill.

Tours

Museum staff try to give individual guided tours when desired. At busy times, however, they can't take care of everybody. Call ahead to make arrangements for group tours.

Presidio La Bahia

Presidio Nuestra Senora de Loreto de la Bahia del Espiritu Santo

On Hwy 183 about three-quarters of a mile south of Goliad/Museum/Open 9 a.m. to 5 p.m. daily, except Good Friday and Christmas/ Adults, $1; children 25 cents/(512) 645-3752

Presidio La Bahia. The name alone seems to hint of provocative adventure and political intrigue. And well it might. This old fort was the site of enough authentic warring and violence to satiate even today's appetite for the bizarre. About 352 Texas men were executed here by the Mexican army during the 1836 Texas revolution, which in turn led to the "Remember Go-liad" cry later shouted at the Battle of San Jacinto.

Colonel James Fannin's men, captured in a nearby battle, were unceremoniously and coldly massacred while they were presidio prisoners of war at the orders of Texas' old nemesis, Santa Anna.

"It seemed the prisoners were told different stories," writes one of the survivors (a doctor), "such as they were to go for wood . . . . etc., and so little suspicion had they of the fate awaiting them. . . . The sound of every gun that rung in our ears told but too terribly the fate of our brave companions. . . ."

Because La Bahia, renamed "Fort Defiance" during Fannin's stay, was the scene of so many skirmishes during the Mexican and Texan revolutions and because it shows the key, dual relationship of mission-presidio life in eighteenth-century Spanish Texas, the presidio is being included in this guide. It's also one of the best

The chapel looms at the left behind a corner bastion at the Presidio La Bahia.

There was plenty of room for soldiers to train inside the large walled-in square.

restored forts and is unalterably intertwined with its sister, Mission Espiritu Santo, down the road.

It was La Bahia's job to protect this mission and the later one, Rosario. The presidio compound was built much like a mission one. In fact it's difficult to tell the difference between the two. Both were constructed in a square with fortified walls surrounding a large, open expanse of land. Each compound had a church, and then quarters and offices were built into the walls. Only the use of these adjunct rooms and buildings differed. Where the mission harbored Indian dwellings and trade workshops, the presidio housed soldiers and military supplies. And each mission was supposed to be supplied with two or three soldiers of their own from the presidio, though this didn't always prove to be the case. Too, where the presidio had four corner bastions for defense, the mission might only have had two on opposite corners.

La Bahia is situated high on a hill, just south of "downtown" Goliad, about one-half mile beyond Mission Espiritu and just off the highway. The setting is placid here, except during week-

ends and summers when the state park fills up. It's an ideal spot for children to roam up the ramps to the corner bastions (gun emplacements) and survey the countryside as soldiers did during the Texas and Mexican revolutions. The bastion in the northwest corner by the chapel has an ancient cannon to further fuel youthful fancies about the exploits of combat.

Though the fort dates back to 1749 when it was moved here (it originally began in 1721 elsewhere; see "History"), it has been restored mainly back to its 1836 era when Fannin and his men took over the garrison and later met their untimely deaths.

Enter at the west wall entrance, which also doubles as the museum area. These rooms were once officers quarters, offices, and arsenals. There are no slide shows, but there are a few recorded explanations of the exhibits, which include artifacts from extensive archeological excavations made during the 1960s restoration.

This is about all there is to tour inside, except for the chapel (Our Lady of Loreto) in the northwest quadrant. But you're free to explore the quiet square enclosure, grassed over, with a few trees and indigenous cactus plants.

Fannin and the Goliad Massacre

Probably one of the more infamous characters coming out of Texas' fight for independence was Colonel James Fannin. He's the same fellow who refused to take his men from the Goliad garrison (alias Fort Defiance or La Bahia) to aid his compatriots at the Alamo. Though he made a halfhearted attempt to march to San Antonio, he aborted it a little too easily, just out of Goliad, blaming it on a broken-down provisions wagon.

That was enough fuel for detractors. But on top of that, his poor military judgment ended up getting him and his men ambushed at the Battle of Coleto Creek (sometimes called the Battle of Goliad), captured, and executed. Of course, Fannin isn't around to defend himself, but the facts don't put him in too pleasing a light.

After the fall of the Alamo in San Antonio, Fannin received orders from General Sam Houston to blow up the Goliad fort and fall back to Victoria where the Guadalupe River would provide a defensible barrier. He disobeyed. Some say he did so because of conflicting orders from the lieutenant governor, but others think it was because he was jealous of Houston. Whatever, he thought he could defend his position at Fort Defiance. Only after it was too late did mounting Mexican forces finally convince him retreat was the answer.

About seven miles out on the road to Victoria in retreat on March 19, 1836, Fannin ordered his troops to stop to graze the oxen, and General Jose Urrea's Mexican forces surprised them. "Colonel Fannin had committed a grievous error in suffering us to stop in the prairie at all," writes participant Dr. Joseph Barnard. "We ought to have moved on at all hazards, and all costs until we reached the timber."

Additional enemy reinforcements caused Fannin and his men to decide to surrender if they could do so honorably. The able-bodied could have bolted for the protective trees but did not want to abandon their wounded. This surrender has been controversial ever since. The Texans claimed the terms were that they were to be treated as prisoners of war and the wounded cared for. The Mexicans, however, contended it was unconditional (or "discretion") surrender, and that they, the captors, could do with them what they chose.

At any rate, the Texans were herded back to Fort Defiance, and crowded into the chapel for several days. Unsuspectingly on Palm Sunday, March 27, they were marched out of the compound on another pretext and shot. "My God, boys, they're going to kill us," one of the survivors remembers someone saying. It is generally thought that Urrea instructed the prisoners be well cared for, but was countermanded by General Santa Anna. The wounded were shot in the compound yard. Fannin died from a shot in the head. About 28 survived by running, hiding, and swimming the river. A few others, such as surgeons, were spared. In all, 352 are thought to have been massacred, though the exact figure is hard to trace. A memorial on the spot where Fannin and his men were buried is about one-quarter mile southeast of the presidio.

History

La Bahia can thank its existence to La Salle, the French explorer who landed on the Texas coast in 1685 by mistake. He had been heading for the mouth of the Mississippi, but ended up establishing the ill-fated Fort St. Louis colony in Texas.

The Spanish couldn't tolerate the idea of French encroachment on *their* territory, despite the fact the new French colony was a failure. The Indians killed off most of them, and La Salle himself was bumped off by one of his own men. But nonetheless, Spain felt the threat was there.

Marques de Aguayo was dispatched to build a mission and presidio on the exact site of the destroyed Fort St. Louis. There is some disagreement on when the presidio was founded. Historical markers at the present Goliad site say 1722, but some historians think it earlier in 1721. It was originally named Nuestra Senora de Loreto de La Bahia del Espiritu Santo (Our Lady of Loreto of the Bay of the Holy Spirit) after the nearby bay. The presidio was inland about five miles on Garcitas Creek, in what is now Victoria County. Now the nearest bay is called Lavaca, and only a small inlet still retains the original name.

The Karankawa Indians weren't too hospitable, however, so the whole kit and caboodle moved in 1726 to a spot on the Guadalupe River (what is now Mission Valley, just north of Victoria). Despite prospering there for years, the mission and presidio were moved to the present site at Goliad on the San Antonio River in 1749 because the Spaniards decided it was necessary to guard the main road from Mexico to San Antonio and East Texas. Thus was the good hilltop location chosen for La Bahia—the better to see the countryside by. It was also located strategi-

See for yourself what it was like to look over the countryside from a defending position complete with cannon on the northwest corner bastion.

cally on the road between San Antonio and Copano Bay, the main Texas port at that time. Here the presidio became known as La Bahia. Apparently the old name of Nuestra Senora de Loreto, etc. was discarded except in naming the new chapel, which was called Our Lady of Loreto. There is a statue there today of Our Lady, said to date back to the original founding.

Things were seldom dull after that. Besides bringing clashes with the Comanches and Lipan-Apaches during the last half of the 1700s, the advent of the 1800s brought revolutionary skirmishes between Mexicans and the Spanish and later between Mexicans and Texans.

During the Mexican revolt (1810–1821) several armed expeditions (such as the Gutierrez-Magee and James Long and Henry Perry "filibusters") attacked or took over the fort. Then in 1835, the Texas volunteer forces took it over, and Fannin renamed it Fort Defiance. The ill-fated retreat and Goliad massacre soon followed in early 1836.

Do you wonder how the nearby town became known as Goliad instead of La Bahia? The Mexicans rechristened it in 1829 in honor of a revolutionary hero, Hidalgo. "Goliad" is an anagram, without the "H".

The clashes and marauding troops took their toll on the fort, and by 1848–1850 when it was sold by the city to Judge Pryor Lea, most of it was in ruins except for the chapel.

The Judge actually used the chapel as a residence for his family! John Russell Bartlett writes of visiting him in 1850, "After tea we ascended to the roof, to enjoy the cool breezes of the evening, and the beautiful landscape which there opens to view. After the moon rose and cast a deep shadow from the ruined walls . . . the scene assumed an aspect of peculiar solemnity and interest."

Museum, Archeological Digs, and Restoration

Old 1880 photos of the fort chapel show the building still standing with walls intact, but the bell tower on its left front is collapsed. The rest of the compound appears in ruins. Apparently somewhere around the 1930s, the simple rock

Inside the compound, the exhibit area is at the left, where the officers' quarters and arsenal were.

This ramp leads up to the northwest corner bastion, where the cannon is located.

chapel was restored and its belfry reinstated. This rough-hewn rock edifice is not an elegant, rococo chapel. It has only a little sculptured stone at the entrance, with a single statue in a niche above. Besides the bell tower, a few octangular windows and Moorish teeth on the roof are about the only other distinguishing characteristics. Inside, however, a huge, colorful religious mural on the back wall of the homely altar backdrops the vaulted ceiling and wooden pews.

Although some earlier restoration and excavations were done in the 1930s, the bulk was done from 1963–67 with the financial help of the Kathryn O'Connor Foundation.

At this time, careful archeological excavations were tediously done before restoring the entire walled-compound back to its 1836 condition. All the dirt within the square enclosure was dug down six to eight feet and sifted and recorded. Around 3,800 artifacts, including gun parts, locks, copper pots, cannon balls, farm tools, pottery shards, china, and spurs were uncovered from nine levels of occupancy, spanning the Indian, Spanish, and Texan periods.

Many of these artifacts, plus historical maps, documents, photos, and a kitchen replica, are displayed in the museum, housed in the west military quarters and serving as the official entrance. One important finding of the digs was the location of the main gate in the center of the south wall, where barracks, prison, and guard rooms were.

La Bahia chapel still operates as a Catholic parish church, while the O'Connor Foundation helps defray some maintenance costs of the fort, a national historical landmark.

Directions to Presidio La Bahia

From the intersection of Hwys 183 and 59 in Goliad, go south on Hwy 183 approximately three-quarters of a mile (or one-half mile beyond Mission Espiritu Santo). On your left is Presidio La Bahia, just off the road. To peruse the museum and the inside of the fort courtyard, go to the west entrance. There is an admission charge ($1 for adults, 25 cents for children) to view these sections. There is apparently no charge to view the chapel.

Tours

There are no guided tours for inviduals. Just amble around at your own discretion. The museum staff will gladly field questions.

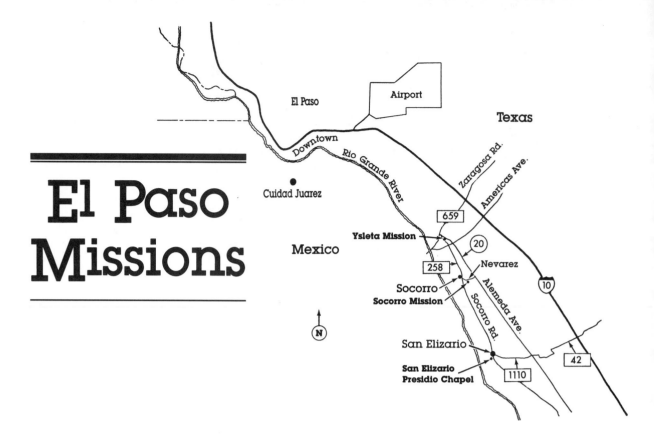

El Paso Missions

That remote foreign province known as El Paso, hundreds of miles west of the rest of Texas civilization, claims to be part and parcel of Lone Star country. In fact, the El Paso upstart even audaciously asserts to be the *very* beginning of Texas colonial history. For years, some historians have ignored the dusty, mountainous domain to the west as if it were a black sheep relative and annointed East Texas with the honor of having been the site of the state's earliest Spanish settlements. But East Texas wasn't.

Even before La Salle's ill-fated, brief sojourn on the Texas coast, Spaniards were "pitching their tents," i.e., building missions, in El Paso del Norte in 1680. The Pueblo Indians in New Mexico revolted that year and forced the Spaniards to flee south for their lives. They regrouped in the pass made by the Rio Grande long used by explorers and conquistadors to go through the mountains.

This El Paso del Norte (the name actually refers to Juarez, Mexico, before it became

"Juarez" some years later and abdicated the name of "El Paso" to what is now El Paso) was where Spaniards had for years come through on their way north from Mexico to look for the rumored cities of gold farther north in New Mexico. Another mission, Nuestra Senora de Guadalupe del Paso del Norte, had already been founded (in Juarez) in 1659, and to this the Spanish fled, forming more missions along the Rio Grande in 1680.

With the shift of the Rio Grande banks over the years, two of these missions, Ysleta and Socorro, and the San Elizario presidio chapel remain to this day on the Texas side. The missions differ markedly in looks and architecture from those in San Antonio and Goliad. They have more an Indian or New Mexican look, well punctuated by the presence of the Tigua Indian Reservation (only one of two reservations in Texas) at Ysleta. Too, there isn't nearly as much to see at these missions, other than the churches, because the walled compounds haven't survived the years nor have the missions been turned into restored state parks. (However, a local Mission Trail organization has obtained some grants for restoration and is actively working towards preserving the area's cultural and architectural heritage.) But there *is* the rare opportunity to see the Tigua Indian culture. After all the Tiguas helped settle and build the Ysleta mission, and of late, they have smartly cashed in on the tourist trade by creating a pueblo replica at the same site their ancestors lived in their adobe houses.

If you don't linger long at each place, you can probably drive to all three (missions and presidio chapel) and back from downtown in three hours, but I suggest you allow more time for meandering about the Reservation, with its restaurant, museum, and dance performances.

If you prefer to leave the driving to *them*, there are several commercial tours, including the familiar Gray Line, available. However, note that these are general tours of El Paso sights and not just special mission tours alone. Contact the El Paso Tourist and Convention Bureau for costs and details. The bus tours usually pick you up at the hotel.

Other Sites Nearby

Many sites abound in the area, such as the Indian pictographs at Hueco Tanks State Historical Park (32 miles northeast of downtown El Paso), Fort Bliss, the Aerial Tramway, and the older, Guadalupe Mission in Juarez.

Greater El Paso Tourist and Convention Bureau
Five Civic Center Plaza
El Paso, Texas 79999 (915) 544-3650

El Paso Chamber of Commerce
Ten Civic Center Plaza, P.O. Box 9738
El Paso, Texas 79987

Gray Line Sightseeing Tours
P.O. Box 9283
El Paso, Texas 79983 (915) 598-8878

Ysleta Mission

Mission San Antonio de la Ysleta del Sur, now called Our Lady of Mt. Carmel

At Zaragosa and Alameda Streets in El Paso/ Tigua Indian Reservation, museum, restaurant, Indian dances, arts and crafts center/ Mission open daily 6 a.m. to 8 p.m./Free/(915) 859-9848/Indian Reservation open daily 8 a.m. to 5 p.m./Museum free, but $1.50 (75 cents children) admission for cultural center and dances/(915) 859-3916

Indians have often been overlooked in some southwestern histories. If not ignored, their culture has, at best, been shunned aside in assessing contributions to the region. But not so at Ysleta. Not only is Ysleta Texas' oldest mission (along with sister mission Socorro down the road), but it's the cornerstone of an authentic Indian reservation. These Indians' roots go back to the very beginning in 1680 when Spaniards either "encouraged" or coerced the Tiguas to come along with them in settling this wild, remote outpost in the El Paso area, or El Paso del Norte as it was then called.

Of course, the Tigua Indian Reservation is a rather urbanized one at this stage, surrounded by pavement and the humble old town of Ysleta, which in turn is swallowed up by modern-day El Paso. But the adobe pueblo replica (called Ysleta del Sur Pueblo) is attractive and interesting, in the New Mexican vein.

If not cowboys and Indians, at least you can indulge in playing Indians at this mission-reservation complex that is only about 14 miles southeast of downtown El Paso and easily accessible most of the way by IH 10.

At Ysleta you can see traditional Indian dances, eat bread baked in outside ovens, or purchase Indian jewelry or pottery you've just seen artisans working on. Obviously geared for the tourist trade (though not unpleasantly so) Ysleta del Sur Pueblo contains an Arts and Crafts Center and restaurant, plus exhibits and sample furnished rooms that give you a look at Indian culture so seldom found in Texas.

All this is within walking distance of the old mission in the same block where it all began back in 1680. This is the original vicinity where the Spaniards and the Tigua Indians fleeing from the Pueblo Indian revolt in New Mexico settled.

Unfortunately, Ysleta mission lacks the pastoral setting of the San Antonio missions. None of the original square or compound (presumably there was one) or even a facsimile of one is intact. All that remains is the restored mission church, surrounded by acres of pavement, modest utilitarian buildings, and the pueblo replica. This is due no doubt to the ravages of time, pragmatic use, and lack of funds.

What is left of the mission itself, the church building, is appealing architecturally in a way dissimilar to the San Antonio and Goliad missions. Ysleta has more Indian influence. It is void of decorative stone work at the entrance and is covered with white plaster, with only the slightest of maroon trim. Its silver-domed bell

tower is its most identifiable mark. The church is stark and sublime, yet harmoniously elegant, with a sort of vague Alamo shape on the facade above the roof line.

The church itself doesn't take much time to see, since the sanctuary is all that's open. But the reservation or pueblo offers more options. You can either whisk through the main two buildings in thirty minutes without dallying or linger over the exhibits and eat lunch. There's also a fine small museum and colorful Indian dances offered almost daily in the summer and on weekends in the winter. If you don't want to miss these thirty-minute dances, call ahead to see when the performances are. Generally there are several on Wednesday through Sunday in the summer, but times may vary.

The Tiguas also celebrate holidays in a big way. Almost any holiday, such as Easter, Memorial Day, July 4th, Labor Day, and Thanksgiv-

The dome of Ysleta's church bell tower is silver-colored.

Tigua Indian Reservation contains an arts and crafts center and a restaurant.

ing, will find them giving dances or hawking their artisans' wares. And on St. Anthony's Day in June, they perform traditional ceremonies honoring their patron saint.

Who are the Tigua Indians?

The Tiguas hail originally from the New Mexico area, and are part of the Pueblo tribe. But they suffered a primitive employment relocation when the Spaniards, fleeing the 1680 Pueblo rebellion in New Mexico, took several hundred of them with them to Texas. Men, women, children, and friars were massacred by the Pueblos rebelling against their Spanish conquerors in New Mexico. Finding retreat the best option at the time (they later returned and recaptured the area), the Spaniards took with them some Christianized Indians from the pueblo villages of La Isleta, Socorro, and Senecu to the El Paso del Norte area. These original pueblo names in New Mexico account for the corresponding town names at their new home, with only Isleta changed slightly to Ysleta.

The Tigua (originally called "Tiwa," but later changed to Tigua to differentiate from their tribal brothers in Isleta, New Mexico) Indians helped build the Ysleta mission and have lived in the area ever since. We first hear of the Ti-

was from Coronado who set foot in New Mexico in 1540 looking for the fabled cities of gold. He encountered the Tiwas as one of the tribes living on the Rio del Norte (Rio Grande). During the cold winter the Spaniards demanded that the Tiwas give them clothing off their backs, and the Indians retaliated by running off their horses. After a truce, however, the Spanish burned a good many of the Indians at the stake. Not exactly a charitable beginning for the conquerors and conquered.

Besides tilling the fields for and learning trades from the missionaries at Ysleta, the Tiguas served as scouts for the U.S. Calvary and Texas Rangers in later years. One particular scouting incident was known as the "last scalp dance." Some Texas Rangers had made their headquarters at Ysleta for protecting the area from the Apache Indians, and in January of 1881, the Rangers sent the Pueblo scouts out to find the Apaches near the Devil Mountains. After the Apaches were beaten in a surprise attack, the Tigua scouts halted about a mile outside Ysleta and camped, for such was their custom after a successful fight against the Apaches. Tribal members came from the Ysleta del Sur Pueblo to celebrate and honor the returning warriors and Rangers. For three days they feasted, wined, and dined. Thus the tale of the last scalp dance got its tag. Presumably some scalps were involved.

When the Pueblos in New Mexico were given reservations during Lincoln's presidency, the Tiguas in Texas didn't receive similar land grants. And they weren't formally recognized as a Texas Indian tribe by the legislature until 1967. However, they did garner a lot of publicity at the Texas Centennial Folk Festival in 1936 by giving then-President Franklin Roosevelt an Indian head-dress.

Today, the Tiguas occupy about 28 acres in the Ysleta area of El Paso, where their arts center, restaurant, museum, administrative offices, and housing projects are located.

The Tiguas have a traditional tribal government, with matters being resolved by the Tribal Junta (meeting of the people) and a seven-man Tribal Council, all headed up by a governor.

Touring the Tigua Pueblo

The pueblo headquarters complex occupies part of two blocks in the old township of Ysleta

The church is the only building left of the Ysleta mission compound itself, and it had to be completely rebuilt around 1908 after a devastating fire.

(now El Paso). Park in the lots to the west or south of the pueblo, a short walking distance from the mission church. Then go in the Arts and Crafts Center/Restaurant entrance at 122 S. Old Pueblo Road.

Arts and Crafts Center and Restaurant

On entering this adobe-masonry, flat-roofed complex, you will find the Arts and Crafts Shop on the left. On the right is the restaurant. Tile flooring, rough-hewn roof, and subdued displays make for an attractive Indian setting. Local Indian artists' pottery, silver and turquoise jewelry, and oil paintings are sold in the shop, plus assorted postcards, T-shirts, and small souvenir wooden totem poles.

The restaurant is comfortable and cozy and has a fireplace. It is open the same hours as the complex, mainly in the daytime but occasionally later in the evening (call ahead for specifics).

The food, said to be Indian and Mexican fare, tends to run more Mexican. Specialties are hot chili and freshly made Indian bread. Dress casually.

Self-Guided Tour

If you want to tour the rest of this pueblo-replica, you'll have to pay admission (adults $1.50, children 75 cents). But by timing it right, this will also include the Indian dances in the outdoor courtyard. They're good entertainment for the kids.

Grab the self-guided tour brochure and start out the back door of the Arts and Crafts Shop. The tour goes counter-clockwise, allowing viewing of the various perimeter rooms in the typical pueblo, which surrounds an open air courtyard full of cactus, flowers, and cultivated plants.

First off, are the bee-hive type ovens, or hornos. Next is the food room that contains displays on Indian food and how herbs and spices can enhance modern cooking. Next is a typical room furnished as Indians might have lived in the mid-1800s, complete with life-sized man and woman figures in colorful garb.

Then look at the garden plot. The Tiguas, like other Pueblo Indians, are known as craftsmen and farmers, adept at coaxing crops from the harsh southwestern land.

Other rooms house pottery displays and a pleasing art gallery. Also in the middle courtyard are the dirt floor dance area and a separate circular structure known as the kiva. This is the center of pueblo life, used as a ceremonial house, meeting place, and learning center. Traditionally it would be built with the floor level below ground and entered by ladder through the roof opening. Normally, but not here, it would also be off limits to anyone but tribal members. After you catch a dance number, about thirty-minutes long, return back through the Arts and Crafts Shop.

But before leaving the complex, take in the Old Pueblo Museum just north of this community building if you want to know more tribal history. There are other reservation structures just across the street to the east. But at this writing, there really wasn't much of interest there, unless you happened to catch an Indian artisan working on his craft in the workshops. The Trading Post at the old stage stop was closed. Administrative offices and a herb garden are situated there also.

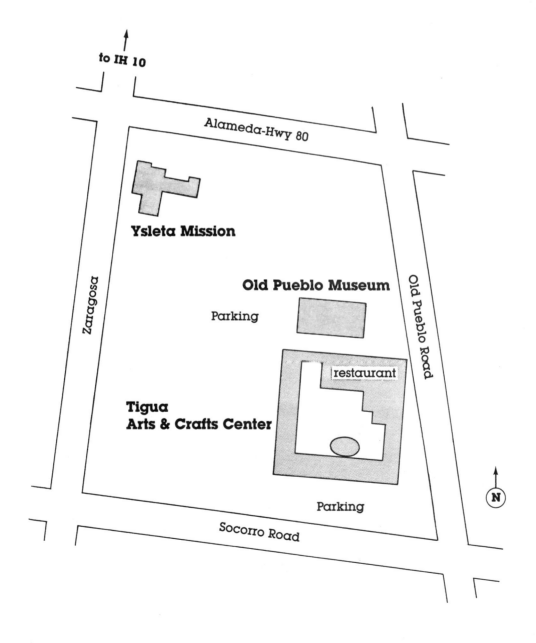

Museum

The Ysleta del Sur Pueblo Museum is an engaging museum, housed in a flat-roofed, adobe-masonry pueblo structure with an indoor courtyard. The structure itself has some historical significance. Traditional tales have had it dating back to the eighteenth century. But during restoration, archeologists and historians decided it goes back only to the mid-1800s. The museum depicts the Tigua history from prehistoric to modern times.

Exhibits include displays on Tiwa (later Tigua) traditions, pottery, hunting culture, the Pueblo Indian revolt in New Mexico, the mission, and current statistics on the Tiguas. Some of the more interesting items are the Folsom fluted points discovered in archeological digs in the El Paso area. These arrowheads are from 8,000 to 10,000 years old. Also displayed are a buckskin beaded shirt and a model of the mission and pueblo in the 1850–1900 era. This model shows no typical walled-in square compound either, just adobe houses to the right of the mission church, and fields to the left.

One of the more interesting asides of this museum is its explanation of pueblo construction and its ultimate influence on Southwestern architecture. For instance, how did they build their flat roofs? The Indians spanned the space between adobe walls with horizontal beams (vigas) and covered these with smaller wood saplings (latias). Over these was laid a layer of straw, tules, chamiza, bark, etc., which prevented fall-out from the final six- to eight-inch dirt covering spread on the roof. But what happened when it rained, which fortunately wasn't too often in the Southwest? Well, by grading and pitch, water was directed towards roof drainage points, where an opening in the parapet and a canale (water spout) threw the rain free of the adobe walls. As might be expected, after a heavy rain families had to climb out on the roof to redistribute the earth covering and do some patch work.

There is no admission at the museum.

History and Restoration

Texas' granddaddy mission has a muddled history that is a bit slippery to trace. But never-

"Bee hive" ovens, or hornos, are still used by the Tigua Indians.

Pueblo-style thatched roof covers a walkway in front of the arts and crafts center.

theless, Ysleta does predate other missions built in what is now the state of Texas. El Paso wasn't in the governing administration of the rest of Spanish Texas but was lumped together with New Mexico territory. This is one reason for the confusion in calling the East Texas missions the earliest ones in "Texas."

As said, Ysleta was founded in the fall of 1680 by the Spaniards fleeing and retreating from the Pueblo revolt in New Mexico (see the section on the Tigua Indians). Governor Antonio Otermin (from New Mexico) and Captain Alonso Garcia set up several missions and a presidio along the Rio Grande at El Paso del Norte, Ysleta among them. Franciscan Fray Francisco Ayeta helped with the establishment of the missions.

Presumably a hut served as the first temporary church. Then an adobe church was built somewhere between 1681–91 and lasted till the 1740 flood. Originally, the mission was probably called Mision de Corpus Christi de los Tihuas de la Isleta del Sur (Corpus Christi means body of Christ and Isleta del Sur no doubt Isleta of the South, taking the name of the Tiguas' original pueblo, Isleta, in New Mexico).

In later years, the mission would variously be known as Mision de San Antonio (St. Anthony) de la Isleta del Sur, Nuestra Senora del Carmen, and now simply Our Lady of Mount Car-

This Tigua Indian pulls bread from an oven at the Pueblo replica. (Courtesy of El Paso Tourist & Convention Bureau.)

A Tigua Indian performs traditional ceremonies outside Ysleta church.

mel. So the lady's many name changes are a bit difficult to keep up with.

Around 1744 an adobe church was built on the present site. In 1907 it fell victim to an accidental fire, either due to lit candles or to the sexton trying to eradicate the bats in the belfry having left some chemical overnight. Only a few walls, a statue, and a bell survived. The chapel was rebuilt by 1908, with Father Juan Cordova doing a lot of the work himself. Today, the church is shaped in the usual cruciform, fairly narrow and small, with the walls painted in creams and browns. The altar is ornate with many statues and a candelabra, and there are some mosaics on the flat ceiling. But it is still a workingman's parish.

In the mission's early years food was scarce, and compound residents had to scrounge for wild herbs and roots. But later the mission had fields of cotton, wheat, and grapevines. Yes, the good padres even brought grapevine cuttings from Spain, and the mission became renowned for its high quality of wine and brandy! The usual mission irrigation ditch, the acequia madre, supplied water. Ysleta wasn't secularized til much later than most of the other Texas missions—1881.

Directions to Ysleta Mission and Tigua Indian Reservation

From downtown El Paso drive about 12 miles southeast on IH 10. Turn right on Zaragosa, going southwest about two and a half miles. The mission church is at the corner of Zaragosa and Alameda (Hwy 80). The Tigua Indian Reservation is in the same block, though the Tigua Arts and Crafts Center/Restaurant actually fronts on Old Pueblo Road. You can simply turn in left off of Zaragosa after passing the back of the church at Alameda. There is plenty of paved parking around the church and pueblo.

Annual Events

Most of these special events at the Tigua Reservation have admission charges. However, the religious celebrations and services observed with the mission are naturally free. All are open to the public.

Easter weekend

Easter Celebration—There are early morning services at the mission and Indian dances performed at the Tigua Cultural Center.

Memorial Day weekend (late May)

Memorial Day—Indian dances are performed and artisans' wares displayed.

June 13

St. Anthony's Day—This is an all-day celebration sometimes beginning as early as 5 a.m. and lasting til 9 p.m. It features religious ceremonies and traditional Indian dances in front of the mission. This special day combines the tribe's traditional dance for new crops with ceremonies honoring their patron saint, St. Anthony. A feast, and other activities also overlap into several days around the 13th.

July 4

Fourth of July Celebration—Various Indian dance groups perform and artisans' wares are sold.

First September weekend

Labor Day Weekend—Again, there are Indian dances and craftsmen's wares displayed.

Thanksgiving (late November)

Thanksgiving Weekend—The reservation hosts more Indian dances.

Socorro Mission

Mission Nuestra Senora de la Concepcion del Socorro, now called La Purisima

On Nevarez Street at Socorro Road in town of Socorro, just southeast of El Paso/Open daily 9 a.m. to 9 p.m. in the summer, 9 a.m. to 7 p.m. in winter/Free/(915) 859-7718

From the side, it's easy to pass Socorro mission by and dismiss it as just another old stucco building found in the innumerable dusty little towns in the Lower Valley southeast of El Paso. Through no fault of its own, Socorro is rather a let-down. Here's one of the oldest missions in Texas (it was founded about the same time as Ysleta was in 1680), and there's nothing much to distinguish it from the nearby run-down dwellings of a poor community. The road crowds the mission on one side, and dusty pavement surrounds the rest. There is no pastoral green or walled-in square to buffer it like other restored Texas missions.

But after all, Socorro *has* survived, as many missions have not. And that's an accomplishment considering how the ravages of time often treat man's edifices. This poor parish and little town of Socorro have done well to just keep the church going, much less expend sparse funds for grandiose restoration. The town of Socorro itself is full of rare old adobe structures, and a few people are attempting to marshal preservation efforts.

Mission Socorro's facade, which is white plaster over adobe, is quite unexpected and atypical of other Texas missions. It is stark and without affectation, some say resembling the Indian thunderbird design. The wall bell tower with two bells sticks up in the front center and has a small cross on the top. The building is flat-roofed and has entrance doors that appear to be of more recent Spanish motel motif. But history-minded architects take a special interest in some of the original construction.

There is simply not much to see at Socorro, except the inside of the church, which takes only a few minutes, unless you want to investigate the old graveyard nearby. Sometimes the church's front door is locked, so try a side door nearest the road, or go back to the parish office building in back to inquire.

As you might expect, the inside of the mission could use some restoration. Rains and age have deteriorated the roof, as evidenced by temporary supports at the altar. The church, which is not the original one and is estimated to have been built in 1843, is in the traditional cross shape, with many religious statues at the altar.

Of particular interest to architectural experts are the huge carved wood beams or vigas supporting the roof over the sanctuary. Many of these were saved from the older mission when it was destroyed by the flooding Rio Grande in 1829. The Rio Grande was always shifting its banks, and this time it left the towns of Socorro and San Elizario on its north bank instead of its south one where they had been.

Perhaps things will look up for Socorro in the future. Many El Pasoans are interested in its welfare, and the local Mission Trail organization has recently obtained a grant for some restoration.

The mission does have two special events open to the public: a Passion Play on Good Friday, and their Fiesta Bazaar on one weekend in late September, honoring their patron saint, St. Michael.

History and Restoration

Socorro's history is frequently elusive and frustrating because so many accounts differ. And as often happens, historians and archeologists update their opinions over the years as more data come to light. So keep this in mind in reading dates.

The Socorro church is roughly reminiscent of the Indian thunderbird design. (Courtesy of James W. Ward.)

The Socorro church is situated in the little town of Socorro, just outside of El Paso. (Courtesy of James W. Ward.)

Socorro had the same beginning as its sister mission, Ysleta, in the fall of 1680 when the Spanish fled the Pueblo revolt in New Mexico and retreated to El Paso del Norte.

Besides the Tiguas, the Spaniards also brought (how voluntarily we don't know) the Piro Indians from Santa Maria del Socorro in New Mexico. Governor Otermin and Fr. Ayeta founded Ysleta mission and, shortly thereafter, the Socorro mission. Franciscan Fray Antonio Guerra said the first Mass under a cottonwood tree somewhere in the Socorro area, but not at the present mission site. A hut probably served as a temporary church. Not until around 1691 was a permanent church erected. After that several others may have been built and lost, due in part to the greedy Rio Grande which played havoc with the primitive mission structures. Another bad flood came along in 1829, and not only did the river wash away the church but it shifted its own course and left the mission site on the northern bank instead of the southern one.

This is when some religious objects and wooden support beams were saved, later to be put in the church built in 1843 at the present site. About 1845 the mission fell heir to its statue of San Miguel (St. Michael), when a Socorro family donated it. Local oral traditions claim the more picturesque legend that an ox cart transporting the statue to New Mexico became mired in the mud at Socorro and thus the statue was destined to remain there. But historians dispute this, pointing to church records that show it was donated by the Holguin family.

The belfry was added in 1847, the transept in 1873. Italian Jesuits took charge of the mission from 1894–1915, and during a greater part of that time period, Father Juan Cordova supervised a lot of church improvements. Later the mission was reroofed, and in 1955, the exterior renovated.

Trying to ferret out the mission's official names along the way is as difficult as pinpointing dates. The historical marker and various histories each have their own versions. But a lot of missions have changed their names slightly over the years, and Socorro is no exception. It probably was called Nuestra Senora de la Limpia Concepcion de los Piros de Socorro del Sur in the earlier years, and then changed to La Purisima Concepcion del Socorro. Today, it's just known as La Purisima.

The University of Texas at El Paso is currently doing archeological digs at a site approximately one-half mile from the present mission, and these ruins probably belong to an earlier church predating the present 1843 one.

Socorro is listed in the National Register of Historic Places and continues to serve as a Catholic parish church.

Directions to Socorro

If you are coming from Ysleta Mission and Tigua Reservation, just take the street bordering the complex on the south, Socorro Road (or Hwy 258), southeast for about two miles to Socorro. Turn left on Nevarez from Socorro Road. The mission is yards down on your right.

If you are going to Socorro mission from downtown El Paso, take IH 10 southeast about thirteen and one half miles. Turn right on Avenue of Americas and go south to Socorro Road, where you take a left. Once in the town of Socorro, go left on Nevarez where the mission is located.

Annual Events

Good Friday
> *Passion Play*—The crucifixion of Christ is depicted, with parishioners dressed as Roman soldiers and in other historical garb. Free admission.

Weekend in late September
> *Fiesta Bazaar*—This is held around the feast day of their patron saint, St. Michael. It includes food booths, entertainment, folkloric dancing. Free admission.

San Elizario Presidio Chapel

On San Elizario Road, just off Socorro Road, in town of San Elizario, a few miles southeast of El Paso/Open daily 24 hours/Free/(915) 851-2333

This winsome white stucco chapel in the hamlet of San Elizario wasn't technically a mission, but it has traditionally masqueraded as one so long that it's being included in this guide. In actuality, the church was only a chapel for the local presidio.

But who cares about technicalities when you can visit this sleepy little town and its venerable town square, complete with gazebo and bench-sitting old-timers, reigned over by the adobe church? It's a journey back in time, only roughly 22 miles southeast from downtown El Paso. And you need drive only a few miles farther down Socorro Road from the two missions to take this in too.

The town of San Elizario is rich in local folklore anyway. It was the El Paso County seat and prior to that the headquarters of Spanish government. Even earlier, Onate the explorer passed through here on his way to New Mexico in 1598. You can't get much earlier than that.

Billy the Kid is also rumored to have been incarcerated in the town, and it was the site of the Salt War in 1877, a local disagreement over the possession and price of salt dug from nearby flats. (Salt was in great demand before refrigeration.) Local politicians, landowners, and priests got embroiled in the controversy, which resulted in executions and murders and even the Texas Rangers surrendering to a mob!

The church, said to have been founded originally in 1789 as a chapel for a presidio here, is a pleasing sight in the more Indian architectural vein of Ysleta and Socorro. Chaste and natural in white stucco (over adobe), the chapel has no adornment, save the slender stained glass windows and wall bell tower in the center. The whole facade is shaped vaguely like the Alamo.

The church is in reasonably good condition, and inside, the sanctuary is much larger than

The San Elizario Presidio chapel overlooks the somnolent town square of San Elizario.

most of the mission chapels. Much younger than the missions (this present church structure dates back to 1877), the church was remodeled because of a fire. It is also much wider and in a square shape, with pale blue walls inside and angels painted above the altar.

It takes little time to see the parish church, but dawdle a bit in the shady park square. Perhaps even brownbag a lunch there.

History

The history of San Elizario's Presidio Chapel is no less confusing than the nearby missions' histories, depending upon whether you consult historical markers or local data. Suffice it to say that when the Spanish retreated to El Paso del Norte in 1680 from the Pueblo revolt in New Mexico, they needed military protection for their missions and a base from which to regroup and recapture New Mexico.

Thus, a presidio was established in the area, though it was shifted about to various Rio Grande locations over the years. Called Presidio de Nuestra Senora del Pilar y Glorioso San Jose, it was renamed San Elizario (to honor the French saint St. Elzear) and moved here in 1789, when the chapel was begun.

By 1814 the presidio was abandoned, but the chapel continued to be used by local people. A flood in 1829 destroyed it, but still another chapel was built around 1840. The present chapel building dates back to 1877, with remodeling done in the 1900s.

Directions to San Elizario

If making a tour of the missions, just continue southeast about six miles on Socorro Road (Hwy 258) from Socorro mission. After reaching the town of San Elizario, take right on San Elizario Road (no sign there at this time). The chapel and park square are located about a block down. San Elizario Road is the next street after the junction of Hwys 258 and 1110.

If coming from downtown El Paso, and bypassing the missions, take IH 10 southeast, then Hwys 42 and 1110 southwest to Socorro Road (Hwy 258) in the town of San Elizario.

Annual Events

Weekend near May 15
San Isidro Fiesta—This fiesta honors the patron saint of farmers. It includes music, food booths, games, and Mass. Free admission.

Last weekend in September
San Elizario Festival—There are music, food, Mass, and other activities. Free admission.

Other Mission Sites and Ruins Around the State

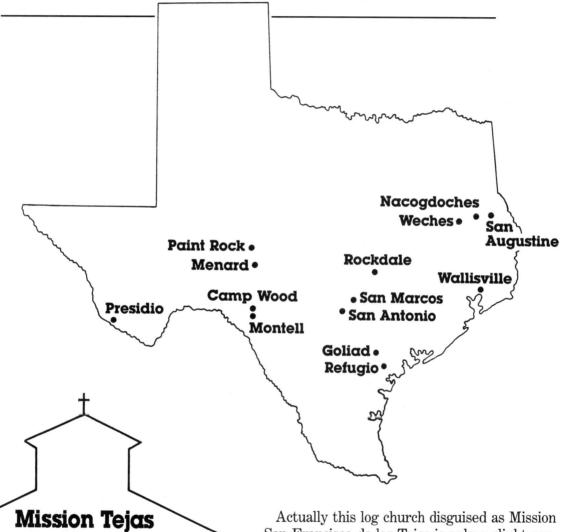

Mission Tejas

Mission San Francisco de los Tejas

On Hwy 21, just west of Weches in Mission Tejas State Historical Park/Camping and recreational facilities, historical structures/Church open daily 8 a.m. to 10 p.m./Park entrance fee ($2 per car) serves as admission/(409) 687-2394

Actually this log church disguised as Mission San Francisco de los Tejas is only a slight replica, and it's probably not even on the precise original site. But why fret about such small matters? The first East Texas mission was built *near* here in 1690 in these lonely, tall piney woods, and it's as good excuse as any to visit this beautiful area turned into Mission Tejas State Historical Park.

Just outside of Weches, the park encloses 118 acres of stately pines with hiking and nature trails, plus a lake for small-fry fishing, a playground, camp sites for tents, and hookups for RV's and trailers.

Keep in mind that Mission Tejas has gone through about as many name changes as Elizabeth Taylor, so you have to keep alert when following its history and various relocations. Ultimately, it ended up in San Antonio as Mission San Francisco de la Espada (see San Antonio section).

History

Mission Tejas began in 1690 because the Spanish were incensed at the idea of French explorer La Salle settling in their Texas territory. They retaliated by destroying the remains of his Fort St. Louis (La Salle had already been killed himself) and establishing two missions in East Texas. Mission San Francisco de los Tejas was the first one, founded by Alonso de Leon's expedition and Fr. Damian Massanet on San Pedro Creek a few miles west of the Neches River near present-day Weches. Designed to recruit the Tejas Indians (a Caddo tribe), the mission didn't fare too well. An epidemic killed off thousands of Indians, and the crops failed. The Indians blamed the priests and became threatening. In 1693, the priests were forced to abandon the mission, burning it themselves and burying the bells and cannon.

However, in 1716, the Spanish again felt threatened by the French and decided to re-establish missions in East Texas. Mission Tejas (now called Nuestro Padre San Francisco de los Tejas) was rebuilt about ten miles east of its original site in the Neche Indian village on the Neches River. War broke out between France and Spain, and again the mission was abandoned. In 1721 it was re-reestablished at the same spot, but under the name of San Francisco de los Neches!

Next, Spanish cost-cutting led to decreased military protection, and three of the East Texas missions requested a change of venue. They moved temporarily to a site on the Colorado River in 1730, but ended up in San Antonio, on the San Antonio River in 1731, where Mission Tejas took on its last non de plume, San Francisco de la Espada.

Park officials are the first to point out that the present log structure is not a true replica, that it would have probably been built of logs stuck side by side in the ground, instead of parallel to it. However the site of the park was chosen because of the discovery of an old cannon believed to have been buried by the Spanish when they abandoned the mission. Located in Davy Crockett National Forest, the area became a state park in 1935, and the CCC (Civilian Conserva-

This is a log replica of the Mission Tejas built in the state park of same name.

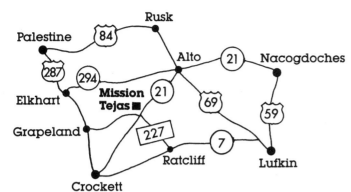

tion Corps) built a structure to commemorate the mission.

The building is kept open all the time to visitors in the park, sometimes being used for church services and weddings. No guided tours or anything like that are available. Just pop in and have a brief look-see. It's at the opposite end of the park from the entrance on Hwy 21. Also in the park is an old log stagecoach stop, the Rice Home, built in the 1820s–30s and moved here from its nearby setting.

Annual Events

Easter Sunday

Easter Sunrise Service—Local ministers and music commemorate Easter. The fireplace usually burns in the background as the audience sits on the mission's log benches. The park entrance fee is waived for this.

First Sunday in October

Pilgrimage—This is a nondenominational service and program of music, entertainment, and eat-out, starting in the afternoon. The pilgrimage commemorates the mission's founding in 1690 and usually falls on the first Sunday in October closest to the date of St. Francis' feastday. The park entrance fee is waived.

Park Mailing Address:

Mission Tejas State Historical Park
   Route 2, Box 108
   Grapeland, Texas 75844

Mission Ruins and Sites

Most of the missions that still stand today, thanks to restoration and longevity have already been covered in detail by this guide. However, there were innumerable more founded that didn't survive, either due to floods, hostile Indians, or simple erosion by time.

You'll see many historical markers all over the state locating former mission sites, but take them with a grain of salt. Historians are constantly updating dates and data, with newly uncovered documents, and this is the reason for discrepancies between the markers and updated information. Sometimes the marker may say a mission was located in a certain place when only a sub-mission (a *visita*) or presidio or village was founded there.

Unless you're a history aficionado, most of these sites aren't worth making a special trip to see. Some are just miniscule ruins hidden by weeds. Others have no remains whatsoever—just a historical plaque. And sometimes, there is no plaque at all, because the actual site is unknown.

But if you happen to be in the area already, or are curious to know the various sites, here are most of the known ones.

Approximate Locations of Other Mission Sites

Presidio

For years historians thought that perhaps six missions were established in the Presidio area on the Rio Grande. More recent researchers think it likely that only one real mission was started here in 1683–84, and that maybe three subsequent ones established about 1715 were merely sub-missions, or visitas. Though legend has Ft. Leaton being the original site of the mission *El Apostol Santiago*, this has been debunked.

Paint Rock, Junction, or Menard

Here's another site historians disagree on. They also equivocate as to whether the mission was actually a full-fledged mission. *San Clemente* mission was thought to have been founded around 1684 by the same Mendoza-Lopez expedition that earlier had started the Presidio one. Some researchers estimate the site to have been near Paint Rock or Junction. But another expert points to ruins (not those of the other mission Santa Cruz de San Saba mentioned below) near Menard as the location.

Weches

Another mission, *Santisimo Nombre de Maria*, was founded in this area shortly after the Tejas Mission in 1690, also nearby on the Neches River. A flood soon destroyed this one, and it had a short life.

Nacogdoches

Several missions were begun in this area in 1716. To the west was established Concepcion (which ultimately ended up in San Antonio); to the north, San Jose de los Nazonis (which also ended up in San Antonio under the new name of San Juan Capistrano). And in the present-day location of Nacogdoches itself, *Nuestra Senora de Guadalupe*, was also founded to serve the Nacogdoche Indians. A marker denotes this site.

San Augustine

The site and remains of *Nuestra Senora de los Dolores de los Ais* (1717) are located on the edge of town. The name means Our Lady of Sorrows of the Ais (Indians).

San Antonio

Besides the five surviving missions, an aborted mission *San Francisco Xavier de Najera*, was founded here in 1722 about where Mission Concepcion is now. Whether it was technically a real mission is debatable. It was more like a temporary sub-mission of Mission San Antonio de Valero (Alamo) and never had any permanent structures. It only lasted a few years because Indian recruits dwindled.

Rockdale/San Marcos

Three missions were established in the Central Texas region between 1746–49. They were usually referred to as the San Xavier missions (*San Francisco Xavier de Horcasitas, San Ildefonso, Nuestra Senora de la Candelaria*) and have a hop-scotch history. Unsuccessful here, the missions moved subsequently to approximately where San Marcos is. The facts have become clouded through time, but it is thought that some of the missionaries and supplies from these San Xavier missions ended up ultimately moving to the Guadalupe River (near New Braunfels) or to the *Santa Cruz de San Saba* mission at what is now Menard. From there they moved down to the Nueces River (near Camp Wood and Montell). To say the least, the natives weren't always friendly, which accounted for most of the relocating.

Menard

The ruins of *Santa Cruz de San Saba* mission are east of town, and the presidio ruins just to the west.

Camp Wood/Montell

The reincarnated San Xavier-San Saba missions that moved to this area were named *San Lorenzo de la Santa Cruz* (ruins are just north of Camp Wood on Hwy 55) and *Nuestra Senora de la Candelaria del Canon*. The site is a few miles south of Camp Wood on Hwy 55 at the present town of Montell.

Goliad

Another mission, *Nuestra Senora del Rosario*, was set up at Goliad in 1754 to convert the Karankawas who lived near its sister mission, Espiritu Santo. Although the Rosario site also belongs to Goliad State Historical Park, as of this writing, little has been done to enhance the scant foundation ruins. There is no sign indicating its whereabouts on the highway, but the site is about six miles west of Goliad on Hwy 59.

Wallisville

Again to discourage the French, a presidio and mission, *Nuestra Senora de la Luz del Orcoquisac*, were organized in this region on the Trinity River in 1756. "Our Lady of the Light" ministered to the Orcoquisac tribe, and its site is near IH 10 and Wallisville.

Refugio

Nuestra Senora del Refugio (Our Lady of Refuge), the last mission founded in Texas, was begun in 1793 near the juncture of the Guadalupe and San Antonio Rivers. It was later moved in 1795 to the Refugio area. Now a restored 1900s-era church sits on the mission's original foundations.

Frontier Life

The Rise and Fall of the Texas Missions

How the Franciscans Carved Out the Frontier

Make no mistake, being a missionary wasn't for the weak or meek of heart. Those crusty Franciscan friars who settled the new world of New Spain and Texas must have been tough old birds, else they wouldn't have survived. Some of the missionaries didn't. If hostile Indians didn't get them, an epidemic or starvation was likely to. There were many hazards to the job of friar, and surely only the hearty dedicated ones persevered.

Take, for instance, the first mission in East Texas in 1690, San Francisco de los Tejas. In the first couple of years, some 3,000 area Tejas Indians died in an epidemic, and about the same time one of the priests died too. The crops also failed, and the Indians blamed the missionaries for all their misfortunes. So they plotted to kill the missionaries, and the priests had to flee for their lives, burning and abandoning the mission.

Then when the friars reestablished the missions in East Texas in 1716, they didn't fare much better.

"Almost from the beginning, the fathers began to maintain themselves by the bread of tears and affliction," writes Fr. Espinosa in his *Cronica*. "The first trouble occurred when seven of the twenty-five soldiers who had been sent to guard the missions, deserted and abandoned us, at the same time taking along some of the animals destined for the use of the friars.

"After selecting the site of each mission, the missionaries assigned to them had to construct their little thatched dwelling unaided; and since no provisions were forwarded, abstinence commenced on the first day. Although it was not the season of Lent, the meals consisted of nothing more than a little purslane seasoned with salt and pepper. Once in a while the Indians would give us a little corn, beans of a certain kind, and some wild fruits, which served to distract rather than to appease our hunger. Rarely was a mouthful of meat available. . . ."

Of course, once the missions got firmly established and going, they became mini-cities and combination churches, forts, and schools, with an abundant Indian labor supply. Then the Indians really had to contribute to the work load, and had more to say grace over than they bargained for.

"Every day all the Indians recite in concert the text of the Christian doctrine . . . in the morning before work and in the evening after it," a report on mission Concepcion in 1762 states. "Three or four times a week the ministers instruct the Indians. . . .

"The labor of the Indians is to plant the fields, look after the cattle, to water the crops, to clear away weeds, and to gather their grain, to erect their dwellings and other buildings . . . But they work with such slowness and carelessness that it is always necessary for some Spaniard to direct them. . . . Some work at weaving and in the forges, and others work as carpenters and bricklayers, in which trades instruction has been furnished them by the missionaries. . . ."

Naturally, we don't have the Indians' viewpoint on all this labor and enforced culture. There were probably pros and cons to the system, as far as the Indians were concerned. They gained skills, tools, and shelter, but had to adhere to the mores and religion of a foreign culture. More importantly, they had to relinquish their independence.

Typical Mission Setup

To recap a bit, the typical mission compound included a church, friary for the missionaries, quarters for the Indians, a granary, and carpenter, blacksmith, and weaving shops. All of these usually connected and formed a walled-in square (or rough rectangle) around a large enclosed courtyard. At least two of the corners of the square would be fortified with bastions and cannons. Close by an acequia would carry water from the river the Spaniards were always careful to build near. The mission farm would be adjacent to the square, and perhaps further away there would be a mission ranch. As you can see, the missionaries had to be jack-of-all-trades—teacher, carpenter, cattleman, architect, and preacher—to oversee all this diverse activity.

Most necessities—food, clothing, and leather goods—were produced by the mission itself. And cattle hides were used to barter for the goods that couldn't be made at the mission, such as guns, iron, and medicine.

Usually only two or three missionaries ran each mission, with maybe two soldiers for protection. But even the soldiers were sometimes capriciously withdrawn by the military. There seemed to be perennial bickering between the religious, military, and political factions in Spain's settlements, each accusing the others of being incompetent.

Most of the time there was a presidio (fort) in the vicinity to give added protection to the surrounding missions. But in belt-tightening times, Spain sometimes withdrew forts, and thus the safety of the missions was imperiled. This paucity of military protection frequently led to the missions' abandonment.

Overall History of Texas Missions

Earlier I detailed how individual missions evolved, lumping them together geographically as you might want to visit them. Now let's pull them all together and take a brief, overall look at the rise and fall of the Texas mission period in general.

First of all, in following the missions, remember they frequently moved from place to place when rivers flooded them out or some budgetary chieftain decreed they relocate. And often they changed names when moving, so that what may have appeared to be a new mission was actually an old one revived. Establishment dates also tend to be elusive, and historians periodically adjust them as more documents are uncovered.

So, it's difficult to pinpoint just how *many* missions were actually founded in Texas. How you total them up depends on your definition of a mission and whether you count a reestablished mission with a new name/location as a new one. Many heretofore thought-to-be missions were actually only sub-missions, or visitas, or villages. Some historians put the total number of missions in the thirties. But by counting the reestablished missions only once and discarding some of those that researchers now feel were only sub-missions, a lower total of about twenty is possible. And this rough estimate of 20 to 30 is subject to change as academics continually update their research and opinions!

To reiterate, the first missions in Texas, were not in East Texas, but the El Paso region. A mother mission, Guadalupe, had already been formed in Juarez, Mexico, in 1659. And when the Pueblo Indians revolted against their conquerors in New Mexico, the Spaniards retreated to the El Paso area in 1680, establishing several missions, two of which ultimately ended up on the Texas side—Ysleta and Socorro.

From here history is a bit sketchy. For years academics estimated that perhaps six missions were then established in the Presidio area, farther down on the Rio Grande, beginning in 1683–84. Now more recent research leans towards evidence that only one mission, El Apostol Santiago, was founded around 1683–84. The others, maybe three, were more likely only submissions or visitas when they were established around 1715. A fort and mission were also founded on the Mexican side, and the whole area at that time was called La Junta de los Rios.

The same Mendoza-Fr. Lopez expedition that had come out of Juarez (the El Paso area) to found the mission at Presidio also wandered out into the interior of "west" Texas in 1684 to establish what may have been another mission, San Clemente. Historians disagree as to whether it was an actual mission and even where it was located. Some say it was near Paint Rock or Junction. Others say that it was more likely near Menard.

Then in 1685, the Frenchman La Salle upset the Spanish applecart by sailing accidentally to the Texas coast while looking for the mouth of the Mississippi River. His ill-fated Fort St. Louis colony on a creek off of Lavaca Bay near Victoria didn't last long, and he was killed. But the settlement set off rumbles in Spanish officialdom.

Immediately, expeditions were sent out to destroy his camp and discourage the French by settling in East Texas. The de Leon expedition established mission San Francisco de los Tejas near Weches in 1690, among what the Spaniards called the Tejas Indians. Soon after that, in the same year, a short-lived mission, Santisimo Nombre de Maria was started nearby. The Spanish had to abandon Mission Tejas because of threatening Indians and hardships, and for the time being, Spanish colonization of Texas lay in the doldrums. Some missions were formed on the other side of the Rio Grande in Mexico, however.

Then France started making noises again in the Louisiana-Mississippi area, and Spain reacted reflexively by going back to East Texas in 1716–17 to reestablish Tejas and five more missions in the area (Concepcion, Guadalupe, and San Jose de los Nazonis in the Nacogdoches area, Dolores de los Ais in the San Augustine area, and one in Louisiana) plus a presidio (near Nacogdoches).

A few years later, it dawned on the Spanish that they needed a halfway station between their settlements on the Rio Grande at Eagle Pass (San Juan Bautista) and their East Texas ones. The way was a long trek for supplies and men through hazardous territory. This led to the settlement on the San Antonio River and the birth of the Alamo (San Antonio de Valero) and a presidio there in 1718. Later another mission, San Jose, would be started in 1720. Hence the evolvement of the El Camino Real (King's Highway, also called the Old San Antonio Road) from Eagle Pass through San Antonio to the Nacogdoches area.

Meanwhile back in East Texas in 1719, the missions were having their usual troubles, such as crop failures and sickness. And too, France and Spain had gone to war. When a few French soldiers appeared in the area, the Spanish fled to San Antonio, abandoning the missions. Like an instant replay, the Spanish *again* returned in 1721 and reestablished the missions, adding a presidio near the Louisiana mission.

Around this time in 1721–22, near the coast where Fort St. Louis had been, part of the Aguayo expedition which had just gone to East Texas, veered to the coast and set up another presidio-mission duo, which eventually became known as Mission Espiritu and La Bahia presidio. This was the same pair later moved to the present town of Goliad. Again, this settlement was designed to discourage the French and protect the Spanish's coastal landing area.

Administrative cost-cutting soon closed down the East Texas presidio. As you can see, Spanish officials never could quite agree on whether the settlements in Texas were worth the expense, and they constantly wrote up reports closing or opening them. Anyway, three missions (Concepcion, San Francisco de los Tejas, and San Jose de los Nazonis) requested a geographical transfer for safety's sake and ended up eventually in San Antonio in 1731. San Jose de los Nazonis took on the name of San Juan Capistrano.

Meanwhile, the Catholic church felt compelled to Christianize and civilize the plains Indians. In the end, this would prove to be an unwise move. The hunter tribes were more warlike than the fairly peaceful agricultural tribes the missionaries had dealt with before. But undaunted, the church established several missions in central and west Texas to accomplish this goal. In general these met with *deadly* failure.

Beginning around 1746–50, three missions were started near Rockdale (northeast of Austin), with an accompanying presidio. They were called the San Xavier missions because of being located on what was then called the San Xavier River (now San Gabriel). Their actual names were San Francisco Xavier de Horcasitas, San Ildefonso, and Nuestra Senora de la Candelaria. Apache raids and the murder of one of the missionaries led the missions to be moved further south to the San Marcos River near where San Marcos is now, in 1755.

The facts are not entirely clear, but in their zest to Christianize and placate the Apaches, the church/state decided in 1756 to transfer some of the personnel and accouterments of the unsuccessful San Xavier missions and presidio to west Texas on the San Saba River at what is now Menard. Spain wanted to explore purported mineral lodes in the area and open up closer communication with its New Mexican settlements. The Apaches, however, proved unamenable to being civilized at this newly named mission, Santa Cruz de San Saba, and the marauding Comanches were even less so. The Indians killed several people at the mission, including two padres. So much for this missionary attempt.

The friars, however, were a determined lot. Remnants of this mission (alias the former San Xavier missions) are thought to have been transferred south in 1762 to the Nueces River near the present towns of Camp Wood and Montell. Here the two missions took on the names of San Lorenzo de la Santa Cruz and Nuestra Senora de la Candelaria del Canon (sound familiar?). Although the Apaches at least congregated there, they never really acquiesced to the work schedule and discipline, and the missions bit the dust in a few years.

After starting the San Xavier missions, Spain started worrying about the French again in 1755–56 and decided they needed to put a mission (Nuestra Senora de la Luz del Orcoquisac) and presidio closer to Louisiana on the Trinity River near present-day Wallisville and Anahuac. (The mission was abandoned after not much success around 1770.)

Around this time, 1749–1755, several visitas, or sub-missions were created in South Texas along the Rio Grande. They didn't have resident missionaries and would be visited by one periodically, rather like a preacher traveling the circuit.

In 1754 another mission, Nuestra Senora del Rosario, was erected to serve the Karankawas near the La Bahia presidio and mission (at Goliad). And in 1793, a little to the south closer to the coast, the last Texas mission to be organized was Nuestra Senora del Refugio. From then on the Spanish shifted their main efforts farther west to California. By the 1790s, about the only missions still surviving were in San Antonio, La Bahia, and El Paso, plus the one in Refugio. Those in the "Texas" district were officially closed or secularized (turned into regular parish churches, with the lands and tools divided among the resident Indians) around 1792–94, except for the ones near La Bahia and Refugio. These operated on until around 1829–31. But actually the San Antonio missions (except the Alamo) were only *partially* secularized until 1813–24. The El Paso missions, being in another jurisdiction, weren't secularized til years later, around 1881.

Why did the mission system decline? Well, for one thing, perhaps the time had come for it to disappear in the sunset. While historians may disagree on just how successful the friars were in Christianizing the Indians, the mission-presidio system had fairly well served its purpose of settling and conquering a foreign land and its people—at least from the Spanish viewpoint. Spain had been able to use native labor to build churches and villages, and at the same time some skills and material goods were imparted to the Indians. The padres had also tried to treat the Indians' sicknesses and souls. And in all fairness, when the missions were secularized, land and equipment were parceled out to the resident Indians.

One decisive blow that accelerated the missions' demise was an official decree around 1778–80 that declared all unbranded cattle belonged to the government. The Spanish crown had decided that Texas was a drain on the royal pocketbook, and that cattle was the only resource to tap. Indeed, cattle were the main source of the missions' income, and naturally most of the cattle weren't branded. This dealt a final economic blow to the already tottering mission system.

Birth of the Texas Cattle Industry

Speaking of cattle, this brings to mind another chief contribution of the missions—the cattle industry. Spaniards like Cortez brought cattle and horses over with them when they came to Mexico, which then infiltrated northward to Texas. The expeditions establishing the missions also carried cattle and livestock with them, consequently cattle ranching spread.

This was particularly so in the San Antonio-South Texas area. All the San Antonio and Goliad missions had ranches, with Espiritu's being the largest. It had an estimated 40,000 cattle at one time. The ranches were not necessarily adjacent to the missions. For instance, Espada's ranch, Rancho de las Cabras, was located about thirty miles southeast of San Antonio, near what is now Floresville. There are still a few ruins left today at the site (near Hwy 97), but the area currently is not open to the public. The ranch headquarters could be quite large themselves, including quarters for the Indian vaqueros and perhaps a chapel. Las Cabras had 26 residents at one time. Many of our cowboy and ranching terms, such as rancho, bronco, hacienda, chaps, poncho, and corral, come from the Spanish.

Resources for Learning More About the Missions

Books and Booklets

There are many books on Texas mission history—some scholarly and effusively detailed, some brief booklets. Here are just a representative few published in the recent past that should be available at libraries or bookstores:

Ashford, Gerald, *Spanish Texas*, Jenkins Publishing Co., The Pemberton Press, Austin and New York, 1971.

Bolton, Herbert E., *Texas in the Middle Eighteenth Century*, first published in 1915, then in 1962, now as an edition by the University of Texas Press, Austin, 1970.

Burrus, Rev. Ernest J., booklet on El Paso missions, Historical Cultural Commission of the Catholic Diocese of El Paso, 1981.

Castaneda, Carlos E., *Our Catholic Heritage in Texas*, 7 vols., Von Boeckmann-Jones, Austin, 1936–1958; reprint, Arno, New York, 1976.

Eastland, Tom, and Fred Armstrong, *The Goliad Massacre*, a booklet, Victoria, Texas, 1974.

Eaton, Jack D., *Excavations at the Alamo Shrine*, Center for Archaeological Research, the University of Texas at San Antonio, Special Report No. 10, 1980.

Guerra, Mary Ann Noonan, *The Missions of San Antonio*, Alamo Press, San Antonio, 1982; *An Alamo Album*, San Antonio, 1981.

Habig, Marion A., O.F.M., *The Alamo Chain of Missions*, Franciscan Herald Press, Chicago, 1968, revised 1976; *San Antonio's Mission San Jose*, 1968; *The Alamo Mission: San Antonio de Valero, 1718–1793*, 1977.

Leutenegger, Benedict, O.F.M., series of translations of mission documents and diaries for the Old Spanish Missions Historical Research Library, San Antonio, 1973–79.

Long, C. J., *1836, The Alamo*, a booklet of the Daughters of the Republic of Texas, 1981.

Lord, Walter, *A Time to Stand*, Harper and Row, 1961; Bison Book paperback, University of Nebraska Press, Lincoln, 1978.

Morrow, Herbert C., *The Mission Trail: History, Architecture, Cultural Heritage, and Historic Preservation of the Lower Valley of El Paso Texas*, a report for West Texas Council of Government, 1981.

O'Connor, Kathryn Stoner, *Presidio La Bahia*, printed by Von Boeckmann-Jones Co., Austin, 1966.

Perry, Carmen, (translator and editor), *With Santa Anna in Texas, A Personal Narrative of the Revolution by Jose Enrique de la Pena*, Texas A&M University Press, College Station, Texas, 1975.

Ramsdell, Charles (revised edition by Carmen Perry), *San Antonio, A Historical and Pictorial Guide*, University of Texas Press, Austin and London, 1959, 1976.

University of Texas Institute of Texan Cultures at San Antonio, Samuel Nesmith, principal researcher, *The Spanish Texans*, a booklet, 1981.

Library Research Resources

Listed below are some libraries with good resources for researching the missions further:

Texas History Research Library of the Daughters of the Republic of Texas is located at the Alamo in San Antonio. It contains material on the history of Texas, in particular the Texas Republic period. Books, documents, maps, photos, periodicals, newspapers, clippings, and family papers are available for research.

Old Spanish Missions Historical Research Library at Our Lady of the Lake University is at 411 S.W. 24th Street in San Antonio. It specializes in the Spanish colonial period of Texas history, particularly the Franciscan missions. There are microfilmed copies of archival documents from Mexico, Spain, and other countries, plus maps, slides, and photos. The library has printed a documentary series of translations of some of this material.

Institute of Texan Cultures is at HemisFair Plaza in San Antonio. Besides a Spanish colonial exhibit on the ground floor, it contains a small reference library on Texas history and folk culture, plus a collection of historic photos.

University of Texas at Austin Library system has a large collection of originals and transcripts of old documents from Spanish and Mexican archives. See also the *Texas State Library* in Austin.

Index

BEETHOVEN MASTERPIECES
for Solo Piano
25 Works

LUDWIG VAN BEETHOVEN

DOVER PUBLICATIONS, INC.
Mineola, New York

Bibliographical Note

This Dover edition, first published in 2004, is a new compilation of piano works originally published separately in authoritative early editions.

International Standard Book Number: 0-486-43570-9

Manufactured in the United States of America
Dover Publications, Inc., 31 East 2nd Street, Mineola, N.Y. 11501